Cell Traffic

Cell Traffic

New and Selected Poems

Heid E. Erdrich

THE UNIVERSITY OF
ARIZONA PRESS

TUCSON

THE UNIVERSITY OF ARIZONA PRESS

© 2012 Heid E. Erdrich
All rights reserved

www.uapress.arizona.edu

Library of Congress Cataloging-in-Publication Data

Erdrich, Heid E. (Heid Ellen)
  Cell traffic : new and selected poems / Heid E. Erdrich.
    p. cm. — (Sun tracks: an American Indian literary series ; v. 70)
  Includes bibliographical references.
  ISBN 978-0-8165-3008-3 (pbk. : acid-free paper)
  I. Title.
  PS3555.R418C45 2012
  811'.54—dc23
                        2011042125

Publication of this book is made possible in part by the proceeds of a permanent en-
dowment created with the assistance of a Challenge Grant from the National Endow-
ment for the Humanities, a federal agency.

♻

Manufactured in the United States of America on acid-free, archival-quality paper con-
taining a minimum of 30% post-consumer waste and processed chlorine free.

17   16   15   14   13   12   6   5   4   3   2

The poems in the sections *National Monuments* (Michigan State University Press,
2008), *The Mother's Tongue* (Salt Publishing, 2005), and *Fishing for Myth* (New Rivers
Press, 1997) are reprinted by permission.

To my sisters, Louise, Lise, and Angie.
You are a part of me—perhaps literally.

Contents

I. Chimeras

II. Cannibals

III. Tourists

IV. Traffickers

Uncollected Work (2006–2011)

I. Prose Poems and Translations

II. Prose Poems

III. Prose Originals

Selected Work (1997–2008)

from *National Monuments* (2008)

from *The Mother's Tongue* (2005)

from *Fishing for Myth* (1997)

The Poetry of Participation: On the Work of Heid Erdrich

Dean Rader

"Perhaps the greatest lesson of Indian poetry" writes Osage scholar Robert Warrior "is that it has often shown us not only how tradition is able to live in new written forms, but that it does not have to dress up in beads and feathers in order to be powerful." Warrior's smart observation perfectly captures Native poetry's ability to simultaneously embody both tradition and innovation. Rather than waving the oral tradition flag, Warrior foregrounds Native poetry's textuality, its written-ness. He foregrounds form over content and praises Native poetry, a la Ezra Pound, for its newness, its edginess. In fact, in *Tribal Secrets*, from which this passage derives, Warrior urges Native critics to take a page from the Native poet handbook. As some of our best writers have demonstrated, Native poetry is geared up to any challenge—it takes on language, ideas, science, computers, pop music, Facebook, love—even other poetry.

No poet is taking on more than Heid Erdrich.

In fact, my ridiculous pun about her is that the only thing Heid does not do is hide, which is why Warrior's claim for Native poetry also functions as a particularly salient lens for looking at her work. I know of no other contemporary poet whose poetry is so firmly rooted in indigenous cultures but so thoroughly pushes mainstream aesthetic envelopes. She dismantles (and re-mantles) literary forms, she merges science and Native histories, she assembles poems from RSS feeds, she plays with complicated interchanges of creation and translation, she takes on the deeply disturbing topics of skeletal remains and Native peoples, and she is one of the few Native poets who repeatedly engages canonical American poetry. At the same time, amazingly, her poetry also reflects an Ojibwe worldview.

If Warrior's pithy neo-aphorism points toward a theory of Native poetry, then Heid's work stands as one of the best examples of that theory in praxis. The twin terms I mention above—tradition and innovation—might seem like opposites, but those poles provide a nice entrée to Heid's opus. For example, in early poems like "Turtle Rattle" and "That Green Night," Heid celebrates myth and the accoutrement of myth, but in pieces like "Wearing Indian Jewelry" and "Hopi Prophet Chooses a Pop," she plays with the literal and figurative aspects of Indian semiotics. Whether the poem is an homage or a wink isn't the point; what matters are the many different planes the poem exists in. Her willingness to acknowledge both the comic and historic aspects of Indian history and story are refreshing.

Heid's fascinating Ojibwe poems are another example of her ability to work within a tradition and to stretch it. Like the great Navajo poet Luci Tapahonso, Heid is one of the few Native writers who significantly and consistently braves the poem across two languages. Heid is nothing if not intrepid—especially as she does not consider herself bilingual—and it takes that willingness to risk alienating or confusing some readers in order to create a new kind of poem. A pleasing number of the texts from *The Mother's Tongue* live concurrently in four different worlds—the world of English, the world of the Ojibwe language learner, the American world, and the Ojibwe world. I've always been struck by how these lyrics vibrate with a different tenor than other Heid Erdrich poems: they are quieter, shorter, *softer*. Take "Twin Bugs," "Basswood," "*Wiisah kote*: The Burnt Wood People," and especially "Poem for Our Ojibwe Names." In these poems, Heid does not so much alternate between Ojibwe and English as collate the two, as in these final four lines from "Twin Bugs:"

> Two mysteries I translate imperfectly,
>
> twin Ojibwe words that now also mean
>
> to wake laughing from a dream
>
> that leaps language from the chest.

In this wacky poem about Ojibwe vanity plates and VW Bugs, English and Ojibwe cruise side-by-side down the two lanes of language's loopy road. They swerve in and out of each other, sharing both interchange and progression. "Twin Bugs" can, in fact, function as a metaphor for a good deal of Heid's poems: Ojibwe modes of speaking and being get integrated into the text; threads of two different colors woven into the same tapestry. They signify differently but mean together. They are the language that leaps from the chest and into poetry.

The incorporation of Ojibwe characters into English poems is itself a provocative form of deep play, particularly in regard to textuality. Heid likes to disrupt easy assumptions about text and semiotics, monoculture and monomyth. One of the most pleasing aspects of her work is her eagerness to make the reader rethink how words in a poem appear on the page. The drama-in-poem "Dancer in Twin Voices" is a fine example. Formatted like a play or a screenplay, the "poem" actually moves more like a lyric, though it is presented in dialogue. It's not a dramatic monologue in the style of Robert Browning—there is nothing *mono* about it—because again, there is an acknowledgement of plurality, of exchange. "Little Souvenirs from the DNA Trading Post" wins my award for best title in the collection, and it also may take home the crown in the Funkiest Form division. Phrases in ALL CAPS step down to standard font couplets, which break into lowercase italicized lines that scatter across the page, punctuated solely by ellipses. Fragment after fragment, font-fix and font-flag, the entire poem is a series of bad (or good) messages scrawled on postcards for the cellular tourist. Here fragmentation and elision create a sense of individual strands of meaning that when helixed together spiral in and out of logical identifiers. What is propaganda? What is truth? What is art?

Perhaps my favorite piece in the book is the wonderful "In House." I had the great pleasure of publishing this poem in a special issue of *Sentence* devoted to contemporary American Indian prose poetry. Let me just say, I've seen a lot of poems, and I've never seen anything quite like this. I hate phrases like *it blew me away*, but it blew me away. "In House" is smart, edgy, and artful. It's knowledgeable about the often-labyrinthine world of academic publishing; so much so it both mocks it and participates in it. It's also postmodernly playful without being too self-conscious or too arch. From a formal perspective, it's inventive but not over-the-top. The lines are crafted perfectly, even if the poem is not itself a lineated lyric. It's self-referential ("This book would no doubt appeal to many, many listeners. / Perhaps readers would want to re-read it after hearing it?") without being pompous. We are intrigued by the voice, even puzzled by the voice; best of all, we trust the voice.

It is this notion of voice I find so compelling in Heid's work. And so reassuring.

At times we don't always know what makes a poem a poem. Its "meaning" can be elusive, its metaphors slippery, its purpose unclear. Ironically (or not) poetry can be a bit like that classic definition of pornography: we know it when we see it. And we see poetry everywhere in her most recent projects, *National Monuments* and *Cell Traffic*, as well as in the "uncollected poems" of the last five years. Years from now, when scholars map Heid's poetic career, they will mark the move from *The Mother's Tongue* to *National Monuments* as an important milestone on her lyrical journey. As strong as the poems in *The Mother's Tongue* are, the work in *National Monuments* is operating at a whole other level.

From both a thematic and a formal perspective, these poems exhibit a poetics that is both sophisticated and accessible. As someone who tries to accomplish that himself, let me simply state how difficult this can be, but Heid pulls it off like few other writers. *National Monuments* is one of those rare books of poetry that everyone likes—Natives and non-Natives, poets and scholars. Sure, right-wing Republicans may not *love* the project, but the combination of the potentially jingoistic title, plus the beguiling Cyrillic font on the spine and cover alongside the faux-imperialist art might have the unintentional benefit of leading more conservative readers to interpret the book as an anticommunist tract. Nothing could be further from the truth. The poems are critical but honest, penetrating but engaging. Of course, there is a lot going on, and not all of it is pleasant, but to me that makes it all the more American. Heid's poetic persona (part Heid/part not-Heid I suspect) is happy to be iconoclastic. In fact, the title itself is both parody and revisionist. It asks us to consider what our national monuments actually are, and in so doing, redefines monumentalism for both American and American Indian publics.

However, what lifts *National Monuments* above mere anti-imperialist cultural critique to the realm of poetry is the formal fire to which Heid holds the poem's feet. Consider the gorgeous final lines of "Vial":

> Rich and red
>
> blood of hunger
>
> bled in fear of
>
>
> the next world wanting
>
> the body whole,
>
> each drop accounted for. . . .
>
>
> When they sell it all,
>
> they'll come back
>
> for more.

Heid busts out the poetry toolkit here: assonance, alliteration, enjambment, and some fantastic metrical play. All those spondees crashing against the iambs in short terceted lines is great stuff. And this is just a sample. From the clever anaphora of "Guidelines for the Treatment of Sacred Objects" and "Grand Portage" to the rhetorical questions of "Post-Barbarian," to the Frost-like cadence of "The Theft Outright," the poems of *National Monument* are a tour-de-force of lyric proficiency and tonal modulation.

You'll find the same level of experimentation and creativity in the newest work as well, in part due to an increased presence of the prose poem. It's a good form for her, as it facilitates what I think is her natural poetic tone—that of conversation. I always feel like her poems are talking to me, and the semiotics of prose underscores this element of storying and talking. Heid's work reminds me of Dorianne Laux in this regard, with a bit of Sherman Alexie, Bob Hicok, and Adrienne Rich thrown in for good measure. Like these poets, Heid sees the poem as a bridge, a mode of connection between author and reader.

This element of connection—at least on the scientific and cellular level—animates much of her new work. These poems take up the topic of cells, science, the body, genetics, and their interplay, which finds appropriate articulation in prose as well as in short lineated lyrics. Many of the poems from *Cell Traffic* are unusually clipped, even compressed, as in poems like "Brain Scan" and "Morrisseau Creatures from the Woodland Painters School." Many of these poems pack an immediate punch. They are swiftly powerful, instantaneous, like a DNA chart or a CT Scan. And, like the skeleton and remains poems of *National Monuments*, *Cell Traffic* traffics in the politics of race, identity, and DNA. No one is asking more provocative questions about who, at our collective core, we really are. By merging the objective with the subjective, the scientific with the poetic, Heid helps bridge the gulf between page and screen, between read-out and the reader.

The poems of *Cell Traffic* love the reader. They ask for—they seek—participation. In his influential essay on intertextuality, the French literary theorist Michael Riffaterre makes a fascinating claim about intertext—that is, when one text references, riffs on, or responds to another text. According to Riffaterre, intertextuality is not dependent upon a reader recognizing all of the textual influences or references: "[I]ntertext," claims Riffaterre, "need not be identified for the intertextual reading to occur." Or, put more precisely, intertext transpires when the reader unveils patterns or modes in the text unexplainable within the context of the poem. So, when Heid engages Robert Frost's canonical poem "The Gift Outright," or William Carlos Williams' poems about Elsie, it is her work that completes the incompleteness of theirs. A similar engagement occurs when her poems enter into conversation with Judith Hall's research on fetal cellular structures, Elvis, the Kennewick Man, William Blake, or even the alphabet. This is important because it gives the reader confidence. The reader does not need to know Ojibwe history or Ojibwe stories in order to appreciate Heid's Ojibwe poems, nor need to know about cellular research in order to understand her DNA poetry. Nevertheless, because her poems enact these modes of intertext, Heid partakes in the long literary traditions of interaction as well as the long Native traditions of collaboration.

In fact, it is this aspect of her work that I love most—how it participates in what I call the poetics of participation. Her work is about the self. It's about the Ojibwe. It's about poetry. It's about the world. And even though you already do, reading these poems will make you love all these things even more.

Works Cited

Riffaterre, Michael. "Intertextual Representation: On Mimesis as Interpretive Discourse." *Critical Inquiry* 11 (1984): 141–62.

Warrior, Robert Allen. *Tribal Secrets: Recovering American Indian Intellectual Traditions.* Minneapolis: University of Minnesota Press, 1994.

Acknowledgments

It is gratifying to have the support of editors and anthologists as I create and share my work. I would like to acknowledge that many of the poems in *Cell Traffic* were previously broadcast on the radio or published online (often in a different version), through *Writer's Almanac*, E-verse, Poetry Daily, Cerise Press, and The Loft, as well as in print via the following publications: *Water-Stone Review*; *Sentence*; *Yellow Medicine Review*; *View from The Loft*; *Poetry International*; *Flyway Literary Review*; *Many Mountains Moving*; *Shenandoah*; *Cream City Review*; *Borealis Journal of Northern Culture*; *Speakeasy*; *Cold Mountain Review*; *Ceide* magazine of County Mayo, Ireland; *Tamaqua*; *Hurricane Alice*; *Maryland Poetry Review*; *Raven Chronicles*; *Great River Review*; and *Cimarron Review*.

Many of the poems included in *Cell Traffic* have been published in anthologies and special publications including: *American Tensions: A Social-Justice Reader*, New Village Press; *Sing: Poetry from the Indigenous Americas*, University of Arizona Press; *On 2nd Thought: Think Indian*, North Dakota Humanities Council, *Low Down and Coming On: A Feast of Delicious and Dangerous Poems about Pigs*, Red Dragonfly Press; *To Sing Along the Way: Minnesota Women Poets*, New Rivers Press; *Traces in Blood Bone and Stone: an Anthology of Ojibwe Poetry*, Loonfeather Press; *Dreamhoard*, Salt Publishing, UK; *Where One Voice Ends Another Begins*, Minnesota Historical Society Press; *Sister Nations: Native American Women Writers on Community*, Minnesota Historical Society Press; *Rhetorical Visions: Reading and Writing in a Visual Culture*, Allyn & Bacon; *Sweeping Beauty: Contemporary Women Poets Do Housework*, University of Iowa Press; *Are You Experienced? Baby Boom Poets at Mid-Life*, University of Iowa Press; *Motives for Writing*, McGraw-Hill; *American Poetry: the Next Generation*, Carnegie Mellon University Press; *Boomer Girls: Poems of Women of the Baby Boom Generation*, University of Iowa Press; *The Talking of Hands*, New Rivers Press; *Prairie Volcano*, Dacotah Territory Press; *The Party Train*, New Rivers Press; and *The Colour of Resistance*, Sister Vision Press.

Finally, Scott King of Red Dragonfly Press has produced beautiful broadsides of two poems in *Cell Traffic* and to him, and the editors of the publications above, I express my deepest thanks.

Gratitude

Sincere thanks to the following organizations for their support, which included fellowships, awards, sabbatical assistance, commissions, and residencies during the decades in which the body of poetry in this book was created: Johns Hopkins University, The Loft Literary Center, University of St. Thomas, Archibald Bush Foundation, Minnesota Historical Society, Anderson Center for Interdisciplinary Arts, Minnesota State Arts Board, and, most recently, Park College, Blacklock Nature Center, and McKnight Foundation.

My gratitude as well to my fellow poets who, over the years, have read or listened to my work and given me direction: James Cihlar, Eric Gansworth, Kathryn Kysar, Janet McAdams, Leslie Adrienne Miller, William Reichard, and Mark Turcotte. In addition, I would like to thank my teachers, Cleopatra Mathis, Tom Sleigh, Peter M. Sacks, Wyatt Prunty, and Roberta Hill (Whiteman).

Sincere thanks to Kristen Buckles, Susan Campbell, and the staff of the University of Arizona Press, particularly former editor Patti Hartmann. My thanks as well to the staff of New Rivers Press, Michigan State University Press, and Salt Publishing.

John Burke sustains me in my work and makes me grateful every day for our life with our two fine children, Eliza and Jules.

Miigwech!

Cell Traffic

For every atom belonging to me as good belongs to you.

—WALT WHITMAN

In fact, some researchers now think that most of us, if not all, are chimeras of one kind or another. Far from being pure-bred individuals composed of a single genetic cell line, our bodies are cellular mongrels, teeming with cells from our mothers, maybe even from grandparents and siblings.

—CLAIRE AINSWORTH
(*NEW SCIENTIST*, NOVEMBER 2003)

Indinawemaaganidog.

—GETE ANISHINAABE

All My Relations.

I

Chimeras

Thrifty Gene, Lucky Gene

For Asiginak

Rabbit glances at the moon,
bites thorns and ice, survives.

Plush with winter stores,
lusty winter boredom,

the thrifty gene makes sure
our bodies warm through to spring.

Our ancestors lived fat
and happy enough to pass on

storage technology that beats
zipper lock plastic,

pads us belly, hip, thigh.
Hard to thank them for this gift

though they gave us luck, too.
Spiral of fate, chain of code,

luck genes must match up
with thrift there somewhere.

Placemat at the Chinese place says:
Rabbit, Luckiest of All Signs.

Most fearful, too, I'm told.
Antsy, anxious *waboose,*

stories Ojibwe tell of you
make sense—

your acts of terror and tricky nonsense
boxing gnawing wind—

but what more worthy opponent?
Just as rabbit jabs, the world tilts

then in dizzy drip of melt and sun
the season finally turns.

We stomp the earth crust,
last trampled paw prints in icy patches.

Warmth come again, we feel lucky,
survived, alive as Adam and Eve

surveying the garden, hungry
for greens, planning to go thin.

Damn rabbits ate the berry canes
down to nubs again.

Brain Scan

Ask for a map
when you marry

contours of interior lobes
color codes of folds

hemispheric traffic:
red light, green light.

You should know ahead
about the head.

Lovely brows (so smooth)
kisses planted there cover

beloved's front brain
sleepy, needy, cool patch

constantly seeking stimulation,
affairs, conflict, passion.

Goes both ways, Lizard Brain—
serotonin drain, jumpy as a bunny,
moody blue.

Between you two
the kids are doomed.

Mitochondrial Eve

Children lowered down a well
so dark the stars shine
even in the day. They hide

swinging over dank waters,
asleep in a net strung tight as web.
They've been there so long
they forget what they fled,
who hid them.

Reflected heavens
in a dark pool cannot tell
whose rope holds them safely
or when she will tug them back.

It comforts them to gaze
at the ripple of astral specks below,
then glance at the hole of light above.

Below. Above. Below. Above.
Mysterious, the contrast:
Let go, fall into that deep beauty or
climb toward a brightness so blank—

This. No that. This. No.
They debate decades, millennia,
then give in to some subtle pull,

a strand of maternal code, thinner than hair,
stronger and lasting long as humanity.

Something of mother tugging all along,
and now they know they felt it always.

Danger passed, time past, they emerge
at last, stunned by the sun, wondering
why they stayed afraid of such things

as enemy or other, wondering
what was it made them stay down
so long.

DNA Tribes

The red-eyed vireo calls:
Here I am. Where are you?

Like some bizarre bio-mimic,
web ads pop up while I email

asking: *Native American DNA—*
What Tribe Are You?

All's I'd need to do is swab
and mail away

cells my ancestors took
millennia to perfect.

And who owns them then?

Here I am. Where are you?
The red-eyed vireo calls,

misleading us to relocate,
following its flight

away from nestlings tight in twigs,
to get us lost in a bog,

asking all along if we even
know our own locale:

Here I am. Where are you?

Native American DNA—
What Tribe Are You?

As if that could fool us,
make us forget the nesting grounds,

the red eye cast ever backward
to the place always known as home.

Morrisseau Creatures from the Woodland Painters School

Frail blue-green shell,
an egg smaller than a pinhead.

Crack it open:
Out pops an eagle
etched in rock,
wings arched against violent thunder.

Crack that too:
Out pops black bear,
wary-eyed and wise,
she digs just the right roots.

I am telling you:
I am a bear inside an eagle inside a rock inside an egg
inside this world.

Microchimerism

I

Nub of human,
shell pink fingernail,
whether you live
or all unformed
leave her body
she will never
be without you.

This, scientists tell us, is literally true:
. . . the cells from her miscarriages, her stillborns,
and all of her children . . . We carry them
for a lifetime. But the cells actually go both ways.

Nub of human,
your cells migrate,
are found at sites
hurt in the maternal body,
and in successive siblings,
even those you never knew,
even those who never knew you.

II

Nub of human,
shell pink fingernail,
she will never be without you.

Vivid dreams in her bed echoed,
a wall away and you felt her,
knew her wakefulness
through the quiet she maintained.

She knew it too and tried
explaining, "It is like she is in me,
knows my brain, and wakes me up
before she wakes."

Darkness so soft she feels its nap
cushion her movements,
still she reaches you
just as your cries begin,
then you two are one again.

Or more correctly,
you never left:
your cells and hers
flowed back and forth—
blood river once between you
went two ways, scientists say:

The waves of fetal microchimerism
are just beginning to break
along the scientific shore.

Even in her milk,
her milk for you—your milk,
a million messages, recipes, connections.

This month you demand
brain grease, complex fats;
next month another mix
produced especially for you.

She should have known
when she craved avocado, salmon, sesame,
and cursed the invective against sushi.

III

Nub of human,
shell pink fingernail—

Who left cells in your mother
that she gave to you?

A million unknown others.

What makes us
our own sole and sovereign selves
is only partially us.

The search for God can be called off.

Now we know:
masses of genetic material not our own
inside us, always with us, like the soul.

I should not
have said that about God.
Forgive me, I
am not
myself.

Italicized lines from Dr. Judith G. Hall, 2002, and from Bruce Morgan's profile of Dr.
Diana Bianchi in Tufts Medicine, 2005.

Define Chimera

She-monster can't get it quite right:
Lazy lion body, laid out yawning,
goat horns of hair,
hot-tongued as a snake.

She lies all the while,
given over to her flights of fancy.

Fancy, now fancy . . . she can do fancy better than glitter on a little girl.
Imagine this and believe in that and chase that dream and you will see,
some day, her vision will come true.

She-goat, when will you learn? You and all your ideas.
Just fabrication of the mind.

Then, too, she is me—she is you—in one.

Exactly who is living an illusion?
Illusion of distance between impossible genetics
(lion heart, goat pelt,
serpent's tongue breathing fire)
and incongruous genetics (twin's ovary, son's kidney, blue-green eye)
facts to your everyday chimera, composed (as each we are)
                of body, spirit, mind—
                                of earth and water, of fire and air.

Now, What Is She?

Bear/makwah or migizi/Eagle. She may never know. Or be both. One doo-dem from her uncle and one especially for her breed—those fathered from another tribe. Her children can claim the Eagle clan. Perhaps that will give them some freedom to fly in the face of what it means to be made fractional by law and looks and the liberty she took in loving a man of no clan. There's no genetic marker, but what if ceremony conveys some other family on her own, what then? What would she be if renamed? Reclaimed?

Blood Chimera

O' my blood, thrumming in my hands,
my cup of knuckles laced to hold you,
if need do.

O' you positive, you plus.
Body, O' Body—and antibody.
Bloody cup drained red from white.

Never a divide, only the pulse of ancestry,
red river surge of time.
Beyond understanding now: my blood not mine.

We, my blood, we body and not body.
Other bodies made in me
now make me.

A thousand dazzling phantoms take me—
none will have me alone.
Never again solitary, never sole.

Body, blood, antibody. Perfect, unsullied, whole.

II
Cannibals

Fur Trade Tokens

And they are at it again—

        rubbing pelt against pelt
               for silver tokens

not even real silver. Trade silver.

Otter couple
        couples on a medallion

        creates a heart between two tails
               about to twine into a helix.

Turtle token sports stitches on her shell

        cracked in quarters she's repaired to represent
               X number of beaver skins

        or may as well quarter our blood.

Who took my ancestress in his arms,

        wore these trinkets of weak metal?

What she traded was labor or
        love and the labor that comes after love.

Trade silver reproductions
        real stuff now worth too much to collect

yet our patrimony in some part.

Parted from them for centuries
            still those tokens jangle in our genetic memory

                    like so much junk DNA.

We hang silver images on strings of beads

                    bead them into dance regalia,
                            dance wrapped in furs.

We go on in our human nakedness

            trading one skin for the other's—

                    fair trade rare as ermine.

All of this goes on as ever
                    as fringes sway on a whole hide dress

frantic motion ascending, ascending jingle of hawk bells,
                            then abrupt silence

mark of one song ending, new song about to begin.

Now, Where Was She?

All curled up in an ergonomic chair, worried for her daughter, wondering if her
mother sat down to wholesome whole grain at that delicate stage (in old pho-
tos, her mother wears dungarees rolled up, curls glamorous as a NoDak Doro-
thy whose basket filled with eggs, not Toto dogs, although truly there was no
place like home) reading email articles forwarded by her sister the doctor:
What happens in our DNA . . . stays in our DNA . . . No, if only that were true.
Scientist says: *What happens in our DNA is all curled up around things called*
histones. That curling up and turning of the DNA require folic acid. When that egg
was created that made you, your grandmother's diet was having some effect on how
that DNA was folding and being methylated. And her little dog, too, curls and
turns and folds, warming up to what has happened to grandmother's prairie
home histones.

Italicized lines from Dr. Judith G. Hall, 2002

Wiindigo Pity

Some think the Wiindigo quite pretty
in an icy-eyed and blue way.

It can sing, offers irresistible gambles . . .
you can understand the attraction.

At times Wiindigo projects beauty, usually in braids,
and howls how to save the world—

world of metal and tar and gutters,
world of earth it calls dirt.

It must hurt an inhuman hurt,
ravening inside, an ice-giant to the world,

panged and gulping on the lure of this world,
world of big words and fine ideas

and the mind always spinning a thread,
brilliant spit of the body

invisible yet shimmering,
strung out to catch what others create.

If it eats another one of us, promise me, promise
                    —we'll cut it in the gut and come out whole.

Own Your Own: Cellular Changes

Tiny robot tools remove
what doesn't work in me.
Blue masks, gas, and a moment's glimpse
of a many-armed machine.
The healers anthropologists
called *sucking doctors*
could pull poison from the body
in the form of feathered frogs, hunks of fat, bone,
or arrow points or stone—
never leaving more than a scratch.
The robot doctors work like that as they
clear me, clean me, delete what's gone
crazy with my code—
never again to worry me, those
vaguely threatening *cellular changes*
to the smooth pink insides of imagination
where we expect our innards to work
in static and indifferent forms.
Except the womb, the best of us, the hot water bottle,
that one red organ we can make do for us,
the studio apartment where we
make the best of small spaces, make a home.
When it all goes wrong, we fix it. We give ourselves over in faith.
Blue masks, gas, and a moment's glimpse
of a many-armed machine shaking rattles
and singing before reaching in me.
I wake up without memory,
thin purple line of incision, a thirst, and a word:
S.H.-H.E. in sharp marker on my belly, indelible initials
so the doctors beyond the robot doctors
knew, in the moment they cut,
I was theirs, I was me.

Long Pig

Girls like Peggy Lee,
bland, pink-faced
blondes, pale-lashed
and pug-nosed, those
girls made cheerleader,
student council, prom queen.
Sounds *jealous a little*—May be.
But now they've farrowed forth
four or five tow-headed young
to boar-broad farm husbands,
and learned to love guns and God.
Now they lean into their bones so cleanly,
not a lick of meat keeps up the cute.
All that flesh was like a lush suit that got
all their wants met.
Sounds *cannibal*—May be.
Maybe love's suckling piglet
wicked out what sweet fat
contained that squealing girl.
Sounds *not fair*—May be.
Maybe their love feeds like any human love:
It renders, scalds, boils down
to everything but the oink.
More than my love—
Less than oink, just O,
and ink.

The Love that Dares

He was made in the Garden,
pulled from the same mud of creation.

He is beauty in neutral,
at times a fine walk
on the thin gender line.

Sexual, yet the opposite of sex.
Deeply companion—
the opposite of Adam.

When Eve went naked, driven from Eden,
when Sky Woman stranded on Turtle's back,
he was right there with her.

God is not without pity.

Seven Mothers

Imagine an engine
in each cell, the furnace
of flesh built in each of us.

Imagine in each fire pit,
information, scads of it
about who it was
first made us.

The seven mitochondrial Eves
might be muses
or mothers from above
sent with heaven's love.

These seven Eves stay with us,
their print within our cells.

I should like to name them,
and why not?
No seven Adams remain
to claim the naming task.

One mother should be Winona,
first born, and one Sky Woman.

One should be Kali, creative terror,
and one is Prudence—yes,
you know some folks are like that.

One Judy, or the equivalent in every tongue,
because Judy just sounds like Mom and
so does Bernice, Maria Therese,
or maybe Donna.

And last, I name thee Eve,
or Dawn or First Light Woman,
or maybe Mitochondria-Mom only,
a name that makes Octo-Mom
look lonely.

Tick Check

Freckled, stippled, brind'ed
as Hopkins' poem . . .
My dear, you must check me,
tick off my moles, arrayed as they are
across the vast skin of me.

Connect the dots and check
each spot. Trace the sensory
path, my melanin-bearing mother's half,
outlining my shoulders, elbow to wrist—
the star map of my arms ready to enfold you.

First, check my one dun-colored breast,
and mocha-splashed chest, the pale
divide descending between left and right,
dermatomes inherited in patterned bits.

You'll have to trace, smooth a finger
along every speck and fleck,
decide is it mole or mite?

Or forgetting the task entirely, simply touch all of me.

Bestial

Open my throat to say, but
what comes out: inhuman roar.

Bear fumbling hunger at back palate.

Panther lust cry and right away we are prey
who lie down clinging, but quiet.

Wolf yearning yip, beyond human hearing;
we might tilt an ear, think we are wanted.

Mammal whine and moan and grunt
all my words convey
of what I wish to mean you mean to me.

Might as well speak dog
for all love words can tell
of fur and maw and gut-feeling
for you.

Menu

Now I shall eat myself clean
off the bone, use up the slag
of last year's holidays and pastry
consumed in the '80s and feel each cell
repeat my past when I eat—
creamy calcium from teeth my mother
made of whey, and tang of berries
filched from neighbors—it's a good day
when the weight goes down and what's
left's made of beer (amber, stout, cheap pale)
'til naught remains to eat of me
but decades of darling caresses like icing:
one fig-flavored bruise from a brutish lover,
a million salty flecks left by love's language,
glazed by all who made me delicacy,
sweet meat.

Now I shall eat me down to clean plate,
clean slate.

Embodied

The soul as soap bubble keening,
always nearby, tethered to the body—

We were asked and practiced early
the contemplation of the soul.

The soul's tar of deeds,
keeping it from heaven
made sense.
It had its work cut out for it.

Body never garnered any comment.
Body went without saying.
Confounded mystery everyone resolved.
But how?

The body, always shifting—
soap again, round and embellished to begin,
then paring down, losing detail,
a crescent in the end, bare.

Body driven, directed, compelled.
Body considered soul no more than a jet engine
its passenger. *Vroom.*

Listen to that thrum
coming from red muscles
packs of platelets, oxygenation.

Roar of real—not yet readable.

Something about the body
I never understood—
always on the outside, trying to get in.

III

Tourists

Indigenous Elvis at the Airport

Indigenous Elvis works security:
Chief Joseph hair, blue-black and pomped,
turquoise and shell dangling from one ear,
silver chunks of rings on every bronze knuckle.

Indigenous Elvis works security:
X-ray glances at your backpacks,
laptops, empty still-moist shoes.

Indigenous Elvis waves me to his line.
A perfect gentlemen at all times,
gingerly lifting my naked phone,
holding the line as I return my computer
and extra undies to my briefcase.

Next line, next flight, Indigenous Elvis eases in
too close, asks, "Where you headed
this time?"
Subtle tango, I lean away, wondering what it is
he saw first gave me away—
My beaded barrettes in their travel case?
A slight turn to my eyes?

Oh, mortification when I get him!
Indigenous Elvis, at security, a third time.
He lifts my carry-on,
maneuvers my hand, gestures me close to ask,
"How is my sweetheart?"
Then against my neck, so my hairs rise
with his sigh, "How's my sweetheart doing . . .
your sister . . . ?
. . . the one that got away."

When They Find Each Other on Facebook

Her profile smile a sideways rose
you recall from a pillow long-ago
—and her status: Married.
Still married.

You *friend* her anyhow
so she sees your buff pic,
the one a few years old.

The membrane of time
that parted you thins and you
breathe together when you type,

then she types.
You both lurch in turbulence,
guts catching up with you,
but when this plane drops

no oxygen mask pops out.
How will you breathe?
Except to remember she is breathing, too,
right now.

Then it's just a matter of who pushes
lush phrases and complaints
against the mates.

Or a quick back out,
—the senses come to—
and confession: Too late.
Log-off or not. It is late.
Too late.

Love Plot

She would say, Come up to my room.
He'd say, Heck Yeah.
She would ask, Can I make tea? I don't drink.
He'd say, I drink. Sometimes. Tea, sure.
No one ever touches me, they'd both be thinking.
She'd ask, Can I brush that hair? Mine used to be that black.
Not sure the next maneuver, but they'd start out in the bath.
He'd stand in the shower while she scrubbed his back.
She'd get her shirt all wet and he'd try to unbutton it. Get stuck.
Never mind, she'd say, pulling open the damp chambray.
He'd say, shy, I'm so big. She'd throw her arms around his belly, laughing.
Clinch is the word that best describes what happens next.
Clinch, then cleave, unto each other, old-time like that.

Little Souvenirs from the DNA Trading Post

A pregnancy lasts forever . . . because every woman who has been pregnant carries these little souvenirs of the pregnancy for the rest of her life.

—Dr. Diana W. Bianchi

BUT IT'S A DRY HEAT . . .

Touch me here and you touch her.
Cinnamon smell on the air—

I've never cared much for Time . . .
You mean the concept of time?

GREETINGS FROM SUNNY . . .

Touch me here and you touch what she left in me,
what ropes me to her—

Mountains made of Time, I like.
You interrupt me, darling.
You need not do so, you know.
You are with me always.

I AM FINE, WISHING YOU WERE HERE.

I hear you always, like Eiffel Tower earrings jingling in my ears,
like the silent snow in the globe,
vivid blue Seattle skyline behind—

You hear me in silence?
Yes. Most certainly. Do you hear me?

My healing hands—let me put them on you . . .
How do you know just where it hurts?
Touch you here and I touch me.

ODDEST KNOWN REVERSAL OF MATERNITY.

Cowgirl purse, leather-worked in miniature from Out West,
stone postcard labeled Artifacts of Ancient Inhabitants . . .

What did you bring me?
What did you bring me?

Thoughts of Kids Interrupt My Work

Enjoying my bowl of woe,
worrying boney problems,

bottom of the pot picked from
my mealy mush of world,

you know that dish—

About to slurp *all done*
when interruption tumbles in:

Joy twins, all surreal,
bubble-wrapped in rapture.

I drop my spoon, my bowl rolls,
they tumble me in pomegranate.

Pip-color coats this seed of self,
this color of joy.

They always dress this way:
rose-lens lovely,

shoes bouncy red rubber
the color of chemical cascade—

Brain flood, red and lit.
Now it carries me, simply *carries* me.

Joy. The finish on each molecule
that makes them. Joy.

Yes, I keep saying it.

Look at this world with its work.
Antidote it. Joy. Try.

Own Your Own: The Papergirl

The whale-blue house
on Sixth Street North
has not yet admitted The Papergirl.

The Papergirl has not yet knocked shyly,
her brown glance cast aside or down
to her Holiday Gas Station sneakers,
her red off-brand Keds.

She has not yet met
pale as powder, dust-scented Mrs. W.
or her shivering gray sister,
or her bent brother, rounding the house,
suspenders flapping,
behind the chitter of a push mower.

The Papergirl has not yet
clapped her hand closed around the sliver of a dime
of real silver, fifty years old.

She has not yet dashed across Sixth Street
as the screen door sighed behind.
The pink rental bunker of the rambler
has not yet triggered this vision:

> Yellow teased hair pulled
> in a man's hands and
> that mother's hand grabbing at
> a toddler's striped tee shirt.
> A human train of rage
> she'll glimpse as she pedals by one day.

The Papergirl has not yet skipped collecting
from the white clapboard three-story
where a girl in leg braces has not yet
had to beat off a brutal attack.

Today she collects there without thinking,
racing house to house, cutting across the yard
where tame wolf pups, loose from the zoo, once tumbled
the town's tallest woman as she raked Silver Maple leaves.

The Papergirl has not yet noticed
only Lutherans on Sixth Street
while one block over Dakota, Ojibwe, Mixed-Blood families
fill roomy old shake-sided American Foursquares.

Now she turns her back on shady Sixth Street,
zips her collection bag shut, lowers her eyes
against the low-slung sun, Fourth Avenue at day's end.

She stops in the warmth a moment to adore
the scent of wet leaves, black cracks in cement,
moss creeping a foundation of rocks.

The Papergirl has not yet fallen in love with any man
but Jesus.
Yet in one moment, she will think,
in the pour of honeyed sun:
Nothing could be better than this.
No God. No heaven.

Then, stepping fast past a tethered Shepherd dog,
this thought will come: There is no Hell.
Everything will begin to hum,
and swell with sudden faith
so she bolts alert, stands fully present
then it comes, that jolt, that lurch,

when the engine of creation kicks in.

Just off the Highway

I could have blown right through
Bird Island, Minnesota, pop. 1,141.

Instead I decided I'd alight awhile,
choosing this place for its name.
Besides, it was time to stop for gas.

Neither evidence of bird, nor island
at first today, in a watery haze,
flatland trick of vision—
the tower elevating grain
shimmers radiantly,
moated by mirage.

Bought vitamin water, caramel corn,
(the local brand, stale) and drank
standing in an alley in a town
so like the one where I was grown
I could have entered any yellow house
on Seventh Street and felt at home.

Moments later, at the pump,
a red-winged horse gallops
in time with the fuel rate:
$2.79 a gallon.

A hawk cried thrice
near the red-capped water tower.
Thrice.

I lied.
My hometown population
was many times Bird Island's size.
More like Olivia, Minnesota, established 1881.

Quiet Cupboard

A yellow-painted kitchen cupboard,
corn, bean, pea, tuna, sardine cans, and
a treasure stash.

Not real treasure.

Our grandfather's enormous red-gold ring
the size of a baby bracelet—stamped with a fancy, looping L
for Ludwig, in a scratched brown jeweler's box.
Hooks hung with dozens of bronze keys.
Aluminum flashlight from Holiday Gas,
red Morse code box ready to S.O.S.
Old watches on pegs.

Not gold watches.

Key hooks looped up strings of baubles and glowing rosaries.
My mother's engagement ring, ruined by dish detergent,
perched on the top shelf, small, blue jeweler's box.
Velvet outside, satin inside.

Not a real diamond.

Yellow pantry, lined with contact paper,
mod flowers in yolky tones.
This accidental naturalist's cabinet:
dusty jars of cocoons slung on twigs, wintering.
Specimens: wild nuts—we called them *pukons*,
stashed above the phone book and atlas.
Dried moths or water beetles curled to
wolf-head neckerchief slides, Boy Scout badges,
rolled up 4-H ribbons.

Not a real naturalist's cabinet.

But a narrow room of mysteries,
opened once to reveal, an ivory blade of bone,
a heron's skull grimacing mildly against
a Green Stamp trading book.
Bones and berries; pods of scarlet runner bean.
Boxes of bee comb wax and inner tube patch.
Collages to greet whoever peeked into the yellow cupboard.
Petrified bison tooth, long white feather with a hard sharp quill,
pressed four-leaf clover, all stashed high in the yellow cupboard,
known to be hands-off.
Accidental still life
detailed as any student painter would hope to arrange,
but personal and ever-changing.

Not a real still life.

But evidence of quiet lives, marked in hushed tones.
Even in North Dakota, days whirled with strife, uncertainty,
DDT, a war in Asia, and unrest on Indian land.
Animals, birds, plants, rocks—they didn't worry about the world.
The heron skull in the cupboard, we prized for its ivory beauty,
and because it might be one of the last.

I put my head in our yellow kitchen cupboard,
tried a long smile, eye to empty socket,
to get back a little of the quiet I'd met once in the wild,
to carry that silence with me, to open a mental cabinet
and sort a still life of bones, driftwood, foxtails,
until I reached a place beyond everyday clamor,
until I learned I could shut out what was just then rushing to my ears,
the roar of the world in its everyday rage.

IV

Traffickers

Upon Hearing of the Mormon DNA Collection

Little Lamb, who made thee? / Dost thou know who made thee?

—WILLIAM BLAKE

Deep in some column
underground, dimly lit or totally dark,
there throb the million or billion swabs
sent in by curious genome-seekers,
wondering who made them.
Little Lambs,
whoever made you
never imagined consignment
to secure storage—
your bitsy cells forever property,
awaiting the Angel Moroni.
Little Lambs,
no matter what you learned
of ancestry or especially if
(really) you are Cherokee,
your name has been recorded
for Baptism of the Dead.
We'll all go Mormon
for the end. Even now our samples
glimmer in the dim vaults,
grow lighter by a shade,
whiten like unto Little Lambs
ready to enter heaven.

Now, Where Was She, Too?

Before the microwave, the little Jack Russell's demands, snow clumps on bird-
bath that might crack it; where was she before creaking downstairs, creaking
upstairs, head deep in a flabbergasted aside: African dance class, robotics,
Lego-mania, clubs and scouts, Jazz pack, soccer prac., aqua jocks, Jujitsu, flute,
Suzuki, Brain Gym, and Hebrew school, Spanish school, Sunday school—a
multitude of acts to enact *parental values* for each valued child. Each to her
own van. No child left behind.

Interrogated Self

Smooth blue stone in moss
along a sweet little stream, too young to talk.

My one flip-flop floats off
as I step in and begin imagining a safe place.

Salmon flip-flop printed with hibiscus,
impossible colored rock—
true enough when no truth will do.

You. You. You. Tell the truth.
What makes you worth your room on this earth?

Flip-flop bobs off slowly spinning . . .

I have ways of making me talk,
of tripping the wire
in my brain bomb.

Blue sparks of thought, bolts of anxiety,
hot sick streak cores me,

sweet stream blasted to steam
evaporates off in little wisps.

No good, I'll never get back there.
Brain already alternating confession,
interrogation. Confession. Interrogation.

Weak mass of human mess, no threat
but that I'm tied to that brain, that bomb.

Streambed dried. Rocks irregular in size,
good shrapnel, killers in kids' hands.

Any place safe can change with a thought.

Sweet little stream daydream, but
cue the tune pipes Custer to his movie death—
or the single, swinging lightbulb from TV.

No one's in this cell but me.

Traffic

The Scientist prints a path,
black tracks melting snow back
over slush, under rain,
beside my own boot marks.

The Scientist explains
grass-rabbit-fox talk:
greenly the grass says, *eat me and you will see,*
we will call the fox.

And the fox gnaws the rabbit clean,
even as rabbit bones call the dogs.

In the snow, others add tracks
so the path blurs, gradient, coded,
like a DNA swath.

The Scientist says there's more to it than that,
more than chemical spirals telling tales.

Cells shift purpose
on purpose.

Snow fills in the path. The slate goes blank.

How? The Scientist says, when I ask,
We have no language for this language but language.

Sleeper

Hum of subway or air traffic
wind in grain
distant industrial noises
some drone woken to and it begins

we turn
poplar leaves
light side to wind

part of us kept hidden
then this roar of something coming
now we ripple together

we did not even know
who we were
until the awakening

we lift and shift
starling flock heeds a deep call

when the phone rings
we do not know the voice
but the voice cracks a code
so we say Yes

grow new arms
attach covertly
attack inside

some map fluoresces: here here and here

we meet in secret agreement
clump up where commanded

cell signals read and replicate errors
fill with active purpose
the map fluoresces: here here next here

she wiped dishes
he drove tractors
we were always with you

we did not even know
who we were
until the awakening

Again, Today

The sky holds still
perfect for painters
breathless, fresh, composed—

As if nothing ever happens
or has happened
or will.

God, peel this sky back,
crack open the globe,
float out its yolk.

Do what you are good at,
what we must want.

We who strain at every peace,
resist what's fair and fresh.

No wonder the sky holds its breath.

God, do what you are good at,
what you do best, while we
crack open the globe,
float out its tarry yolk.

Cold Climate

In answer to your unasked question:
because this snow is brightness,
because this brightness fills them,
because of them the human scent in darkness,
enfolding arms, wild dreams in beastly sleep, power in hunger, defiance
when glittering atoms
freeze in wind,
melt in them.

Because I claim cold as my own, as our force. Beauty.

Beauty who wants only to be worthy of herself,
wants to contain terror or terribleness, some threat.

She whistles all around us now, dazzles in drifts,
faceted particles, blasted across oceans, blown two thousand miles and more.
She awaits her day in every one of us.

Beauty says she wants to be worthy of herself,
be the breath that opens O's, pulls brilliant transparence
straight to the butterfly in a child's throat
to lodge and cause, lodge and grow.

Damn, damn, damn-it. Yes.
Because I have loved her icy ruthlessness.

Two Sides

Two huge spruce trees watch over us.
The phone rings and rings and we won't answer.
Our relative speaks in perfect needs:
No home.
Cold.
Money.

His shy eyes, his sly white smile, his brilliance as a boy.

Two huge spruce trees watch over us.
Home.
Safe.
Warm.

Say *no* and it comes out choked.
Tell him you love him.
Ask him not to call anymore.
Hang up.

Tent strung between little cedars, thirty years ago:
Boys sleep like bears.
But you are cold, too cold to sleep.
He rolls his back to you, gives you warmth.
He boils a dozen eggs. You eat all week.
He hauls the water, the wood.
Somehow finds beer.

Two huge spruce trees watch over you now.
The phone rings and rings and you try not to answer.
Someone you love calls and calls.
Your relative speaks in perfect needs: cold, alone, money.

He's living in a park, the weather's changed,
he can pay you back.
You give in.

Tell him: *Don't call any more.*

Two huge spruce trees watch over you,
your safe, warm, home.

Windows cracked in parties past let in whistling drafts.
Plumbing demands immediate funding,
so plastic seal the glass another winter.

Last hundred you'll ever send him.

The split glass attracts your eye
when the phone rings.
Let it ring and ring.
Let your husband answer with:
Please don't call her again.

After that you get quiet, quiet, quiet, for almost a day.

Outside a trendy shop, your kids
offer all their change
to a guy with cool high-tech prosthetics.
His cardboard sign says IRAQ VET.
You tell the kids:
We are two sides of the same life.

Dozens of calls are nothing.
Nothing to your shelter
under enormous spruce,
paying enormous taxes,
playing your side of this one whole
—halved and split—
but same life.

The phone does not ring
and does not ring
and does not ring
until you do not notice it not ringing.

Paint These Streets

For Frank Big Bear

Paint these streets, paint them over.

Paint grass acid green over gray asphalt,
hot orange rivers over white chalk marks,
indigo clouds over yellow police tape.

Paint these streets.
Paint them bright.

Where those dive-bars once bled out tumbling figures,
in senseless colors, and dull shades of death in the alley,
under the bridge, beside the highway—paint it over.
Paint it *all over*.

Paint it so it lights up—sends fear howling off and away,
like the monster dog it is, yelping at fire, heart's passion, action.

Paint these streets.
Paint them alive.

Where ones we loved once stumbled, dying senselessly,
drained to blank canvasses—those very stoops, curbs, rails:
Paint them full, vibrating with strokes of purple, pink, cerise.

Paint their faces.
Paint them lit from within, composed of fantastic leaves,
shards of jewels,
cut-glass beads,
and the radiance of survival, of a people thriving.

Paint these streets, paint them over.
Tell another story,
one that does not forget what formed the muddy storm

in the background, the contrast to today's lightning strikes—
organized bolts of energy, all our work,
what it takes to transform.

Paint these streets.
Paint them over with vivid possibilities.
Neon green, brilliant blue—day-glo lives striding home,
                              where we *are* home,
                              in the strobe
                              that lights up ordinary lives
                              in work, in art, in motion.

Uncollected Works
(2006–2011)

I

Prose Poems and Translations

This section begins with a series of four prose poems, each followed by the results of a collaborative project with poet and Ojibwe language scholar Dr. Margaret Noori. In each set of poems Heid Erdrich's original prose poem appears first in the series. The poems that follow are translated by Margaret Noori in a three-step manner meant to reveal the process: first into Ojibwe in a literal transcription that allows a line-by-line reading, then into Ojibwe alone in a poetic re-expression of the work, and finally back into English, translating the Ojibwe re-expression so as to note interesting tensions between Ojibwe and English.

The Shapes We Make

Letters, yes, printing some sentiment. Spelling it out together. Bent this way, curved that way. O we make and H. Hand in hand. H. You raise your arms, an X of joy. O we two and H. Hand in hand. H.

The Shapes We Make /
Ezhi-Zhibiigeyaang /
The Way We Write

Translation and re-expression by Margaret Noori

I

Letters, yes, printing some sentiment.
Nd'ozhibii'iganankemi, enya, nd'enendamobiigemi.
(We make letters, yes, we write our thoughts.)

Spelling it out together.
Nd'maamwiikidowinankemi.
(We make words to say together.)

Bent this way, curved that way.
Waaginaaminid, zhiibiiga'aminid
(We bend them, stretch them.)

O we make and H.
O miinwaa H.
(O and H.)

Hand in hand. H.
Nd'ojibwemozhaaganaashibiigemi. H.
(We write Ojibberish. H.)

You raise your arms, an X of joy.
Nd'ombinikenimi. Nd'minawaazhogankemi. X.
(We raise our arms. We make a bridge of joy. X.)

O we two and H.
Nd'niizhimi—O miinwaa H.
(We are a pair—O and H.)

Hand in hand. H.
Nd'chimookaniishinaabebiigemi. H.
(We write AmerAnishinaabe. H.)

II

Nd'ozhibii'iganankemi, enya, nd'enendamobiigemi.
Nd'maamwiikidowinankemi.
Waaginaaminid, zhiibiiga'aminid
O miinwaa H.
Nd'ojibwemozhaaganaashibiigemi. H.
Nd'ombinikenimi. Nd'minawaazhogankemi. X.
Nd'niizhimi—O miinwaa H.
Nd'chimookaniishinaabebiigemi. H.

III

We make letters, yes, we write our thoughts.

We make words to say together.

We bend them, stretch them.

O and H.

We write Ojibberish. H.

We raise our arms. We make a bridge of joy. X.

We are a pair—O and H.

We write AmerAnishinaabe. H.

How We Walk

Though the snow won't go and the ice takes a bite, he walks me daily. We stalk
our urban pond, city buildings at one shoulder and gentle waters at the other.
We walk and talk of work, laugh about the kids, then get to the business of
money. Money this and money that, enough and we'll be OK, and money,
money, money, until he cries "Look! Mink!" Two mink, black and burnished
against the white, frozen pond, leaping straight up and out, taking turns in
hot pursuit through crusted snow. We run to the melting edge to watch them
tumble, bouncing, across a thin sheet of ice so bright our eyes smart and
strain. They vanish at the island's edge. We walk on, amazed, full of joy. We talk
of mink tracks, ice and (a little) about money.

His eye saves me, brings me beauty daily, spots the tracks, the eggshell, the
eagle as it passes, something of wonder every day. We walk this way.

How We Walk /
Ezhi-bimoseyaang /
The Way We Walk
Translation and re-expression by Margaret Noori

I

Though the snow won't go and the ice takes a bite, he walks me daily.
Epiichi geyabi zookpoomigad, miinwaa wiindigog noondaagaaziwag,
wiijibimoseyaang.
(While it still snows, and the wiindigos howl, we walk together.)

We stalk our urban pond, city buildings at one shoulder and gentle waters at
the other.
Ganawaabandaminid odena-zaagaa'igens, jiigabiig, besho waakaa'iganan,
nisawayi'ii wiijigaabawiyaang.
(We watch the city pond, near the water, near the city structures, we stand
together between.)

We walk and talk of work, laugh about the kids, then get to the business of
money.
Nd'bwaachidimi. Nd'baapimi. Nda'dibaadaaminan nokiiwinan miinwaa
zhooniyaa miinwaa dibaajimaangidwa, niijaanisinaanig.
(We visit. We laugh. We talk of work and money and we talk of our children.)

Money this and money that, enough and we'll be OK, and money, money,
money,
Zhooniyaa, zhoozhoozhooniyaa, zhibiiaaminid, zhiibiiga'aminid, kina gego da
niishin ina?
(Money, mon-mon-money, we write it, we stretch it, will it all work out?)

until he cries "Look! Mink!"
Miidash noondaagazi, "Nishke! Zhaangweshiwag iwedi!"
(Then he cries out, "Look! Mink over there!")

Two mink, black and burnished against the white, frozen pond,
Niizh zhaangweshiwag, miskomaakade'aazowag aankaaj waabshkigashkadinibi
(Two minks, they are a red-black color beside white frozen water.)

leaping straight up and out, taking turns in hot pursuit through crusted snow.
Gwaayakbagwaashkinewag be-bezhig babaaminizhadizowag gooning.
(Straight up they jump, one at a time chasing one another in the snow.)

We run to the melting edge to watch them tumble, bouncing,
Nd'jigewebatoomi epiichi didibibizowaad, zhooshkwaadewaad.
(We walk along the edge of the beach while they roll and skate.)

across a thin sheet of ice so bright our eyes smart and strain.
Mii nd'ganawaabamaanaanig aayaawaad waaseyaabibagaakwadin zaagaa'igens.
(Then we watch them on the bright, thin, frozen pond.)

They vanish at the island's edge.
Nikeye miinising ni maajaawag.
(In the direction of the island they leave.)

We walk on, amazed, full of joy.
Bimoseyaang, minotaagoziyaang, gichinendamoyaang.
(We walk, amazed and thrilled.)

We talk of mink tracks, ice and (a little) about money.
Nda'dibaadaaminan zhaangweshi-bimikawaanan, miinwaa zhooniyaa baangii
eta igo.
(We talk about mink tracks and money just a little.)

His eye saves me, brings me beauty daily,
Nd'naagadawenimig pii naagadawendanan
(He cares for me when he cares for them,)

spots the tracks, the eggshell, the eagle as is passes,
bimikawaanan, waawaanoon, migizi-miikanan ishpeming aayaayaang.
(the tracks, the eggs, the eagle's path above us.)

something of wonder every day.
Ensa giizhigad, gego ginaajiwan.
(Every day something beautiful.)

We walk this way.
Mii sa ezhi-bimoseyaang.
(This is the way we walk.)

II

Epiichi geyabi zookpoomigad, miinwaa wiindigog noondaagaaziwag,
wiijibimoseyaang.
Ganawaabandaminid odena-zaagaa'igens, jiigabiig, besho waakaa'iganan,
nisawayi'ii wiijigaabawiyaang.
Nd'bwaachidimi. Nd'baapimi. Nda'dibaadaaminan nokiiwinan miinwaa
zhooniyaa miinwaa dibaajimaangidwa, niijaanisinaanig.
Zhooniyaa, zhoozhoozhooniyaa, zhibiiaaminid, zhiibiiga'aminid, kina gego da
niishin ina?
Miidash noondaagazi, "Nishke! Zhaangweshiwag iwedi!"
Niizh zhaangweshiwag, miskomaakade'aazowag aankaaj waabshkigashkadinibi
Gwaayakbagwaashkinewag be-bezhig babaaminizhadizowag gooning.
Nd'jigewebatoomi epiichi didibibizowaad, zhooshkwaadewaad.
Mii nd'ganawaabamaanaanig aayaawaad waaseyaabibagaakwadin zaagaa'igens.
Nikeye miinising ni maajaawag.
Bimoseyaang, minotaagoziyaang, gichinendamoyaang.
Nda'dibaadaaminan zhaangweshi-bimikawaanan, miinwaa zhooniyaa baangii
eta igo.
Nd'naagadawenimig pii naagadawendanan
bimikawaanan, waawaanoon, migizi-miikanan ishpeming aayaayaang.
Ensa giizhigad, gego ginaajiwan.
Mii sa ezhi-bimoseyaang.

III

While it still snows, and the wiindigos howl, we walk together.
We watch the city pond, near the water, near the city structures, we stand
together between.
We visit. We laugh. We talk of work and money and we talk of our children.
Money, mon-mon-money, we write it, we stretch it, will it all work out?

Then he cries out, "Look! Mink over there!"
Two minks, they are a red-black color beside white frozen water.
Straight up they jump, one at a time chasing one another in the snow.

We walk along the edge of the beach while they roll and skate.

Then we watch them on the bright, thin, frozen pond.

In the direction of the island they leave.

We walk, amazed and thrilled.

We talk about mink tracks and money just a little.

He cares for me when he cares for them,
the tracks, the eggs, the eagle's path above us.
Every day something beautiful.

This is the way we walk.

How We Talk

In front of the kids, as if nothing is sacred and everything is—kids who put
up a Christmas tree, put down tobacco at first thunder, visit Ganesh and
household gods, Buddhist shrines, and wonder if Jesus is some kind of benign
zombie. We've made a mess and may be fundamentalists yet. Or *prey for cults*
as Grandma said of unbaptized babies. My guess is she got them wet on a stroll
past the church one day or used the tub. She always had arcane Church Law
down pat: Baptism of Desire.

*See the eagle looking for good people? No wait. I think that one has its eye on our
tasty little dog . . . Creation is glorious, we should thank creation for including us . . .
We can bring flowers for the shrine, sure . . . You can't chant just any old chant . . .
The good news is there's no Hell, the bad news is there may be no Heaven, either.*

The way we talk, in front of the kids, as if nothing and everything were sacred
all at once.

How We Talk /
Ezhi-gaagiigidoyaang /
The Way We Talk

I

In front of the kids,
Pii niijaanisag beshowag, gaagiigidoyaang
(When the children are near, we talk,)

as if nothing is sacred and everything is—
kaa gego chipiitendaasiin miinwaa kina gego chipiitendaan
(nothing is held in high regard and everything is held in high regard—)

kids who put up a Christmas tree,
niijaanisinaanig Nibaanamegiizhigadmitigkewag
(our children who make a Christmas tree,)

put down tobacco at first thunder,
sema bagosendaamowaad pii nimkiikaamagad
(they offer tobacco when it thunders,)

visit Ganesh and household gods, Buddhist shrines,
mawadishaawad Jejiibajikiimanido ednokiid, izhaawaad Buddha anamegamig.
(they visit the Elephant God where he lives, they go to places of prayer for
Buddha,)

and wonder if Jesus is some kind of benign zombie.
mii enendamowaad Paguk gonemaa Zhesus aawed.
(then they think Jesus is maybe a Paguk.)

We've made a mess and maybe fundamentalists yet.
Gonemaa nd'giinaadizimi miinwaa gaawiin debwetaasiiiyangidwa
(Maybe we are crazy and they don't believe us.)

Or *prey for cults* as Grandma said of unbaptized babies.
E-kidod gokomis, makadewikonayewag wii noojawad gaawiin maashi
ziigandawsiiwaa binoojiinsag
(Grandma says, the black-robes will hunt the unbaptized babies.)

My guess is she got them wet on a stroll past the church one day or used the
tub.
Endigwenh o'gii chitwaagiziibiiginaan epichii bimbatoowaad shweying
namagamig, maage biinji giiziinaagaanan.
(I wonder if she gave them a holy bath on a stroll behind the church or later in
the tub.)

She always had arcane Church Law down pat: Baptism of Desire.
Pane gwa nitaanisidotaan chitwaanakinigewinan: Ziigandawi-Zoongi-
Zaagidiwin
(She always understood the holy laws: Baptism of the Strongest Love.)

See the eagle looking for good people?
G'waabamaa ina, migizi naandawaabamawaa minobimaadizijig?
(Do you see, the eagle looking for good people?)

No wait.
Bekaa.
(Wait.)

I think that one has its eye on our tasty little dog . . .
Bezhig ganawaabi minopogwazi nimookajiins . . .
(One is watching our tasty puppy . . .)

Creation is glorious,
Chidebenjiged chiminoaayaad.
(Creation is glorious.)

We should thank creation for including us . . .
Aabdeg n'da miigwetchaanan maampii aayaang . . .
(We should give thanks that we are here. . .)

We can bring flowers for the shrine, sure . . .
Waawaaskonan biidoonaaminan anamadopwining, eh . . .
(We bring flowers to the prayer-table, sure . . .)

You can't chant just any old chant . . .
Gegwa nagamoken majinagamowin . . .
(Don't sing the wrong song . . .)

The good news is there's no Hell,
Debwemigad, gaawiin tesiinon Chi-shkode,
(It's true there is no Hell,)

the bad news is there may be no Heaven, either.
miinwaa debwemigad gonemaa gaawiin tesiinon Chitwaa-giizhigong.
(and it may also be true there is no Heaven.)

The way we talk, in front of the kids,
Ezhi-gaagiigidoyaang, pii niijaanisag beshowag
(The way we talk when the children are near,)

as if nothing and everything were sacred all at once.
kaa gego chipiitendaasiin miinwaa kina gego chipiitendaan.
(as if nothing is held in high regard and everything is held in high regard.)

II

Pii niijaanisag beshowag, gaagiigidoyaang
kaa gego chipiitendaasiin miinwaa kina gego chipiitendaan
niijaanisinaanig Nibaanamegiizhigadmitigkewag
sema bagosendaamowaad pii nimkiikaamagad
mawadishaawad Jejiibajikiimanido ednokiid, izhaawaad Buddha anamegamig.
mii enendamowaad Paguk gonemaa Zhesus aawed.

Gonemaa nd'giinaadizimi miinwaa gaawiin debwetaasiiiyangidwa
E-kidod gokomis, makadewikonayewag wii noojawad gaawiin maashi
ziigandawsiiwaa binoojiinsag
Endigwenh o'gii chitwaagiziibiiginaan epichii bimbatoowaad shweying
namagamig, maage biinji giiziinaagaanan.
Pane gwa nitaanisidotaan chitwaanakinigewinan: Ziigandawi-Zoongi-
Zaagidiwin

G'waabamaa ina, migizi naandawaabamawaa minobimaadizijig?
Bekaa

Bezhig ganawaabi minopogwazi nimookajiins . . .
Chidebenjiged chiminoaayaad.
Aabdeg n'da miigwetchaanan maampii aayaang . . .
Waawaaskonan biidoonaaminan anamadopwining, eh . . .
Gegwa nagamoken majinagamowin . . .
Debwemigad, gaawiin tesiinon Chi-shkode,
miinwaa debwemigad gonemaa gaawiin tesiinon Chitwaa-giizhigong.

Ezhi-gaagiigidoyaang, pii niijaanisag beshowag
kaa gego chipiitendaasiin miinwaa kina gego chipiitendaan.

III

When the children are near, we talk,
nothing is held in high regard and everything is held in high regard—

our children who make a Christmas tree,
they offer tobacco when it thunders,

they visit the Elephant God where he lives, they go to places of prayer for Buddha,
then they think Jesus is maybe a Paguk.

Maybe we are crazy and they don't believe us.
Grandma says, the black-robes will hunt the unbaptized babies.
I wonder if she gave them a holy bath on a stroll behind the church or later in
the tub.
She always understood the holy laws: Baptism of the Strongest Love.

Do you see, the eagle looking for good people?
Wait.
One is watching our tasty puppy . . .
Creation is glorious.
We should give thanks that we are here. . .
We bring flowers to the prayer-table, sure . . .
Don't sing the wrong song . . .

It's true there is no Hell,
and it may also be true there is no Heaven.

The way we talk when the children are near,
as if nothing is held in high regard and everything is held in high regard.

How We Eat

Hot from the pan, green and garlicky—all the energy of sun turned to leaf and ours to eat. What a bear can eat, we can eat. If, lost in the wilds, we don't find a bear, we can follow raccoon's paws printing a menu in mud—nest eggs and berries, with minnows to finish. Or dig for our dinner in the dark like raccoon going for grubs in stumps. Still, we cannot be sure of everything he eats. We do not know every root, cannot trust those people. Winter roots, round and pale cheeked, drawn through earth to the moon, heave up just enough to see the moon and say, softly so we can just hear: *She is not our kind—but how kind her face. How far off and hungry her look.*

How We Eat /
Ezhi-wiisiniyaang /
The Way We Eat

Translation and re-expression by Margaret Noori

I

Hot from the pan, green and garlicky
Gizhi-ozhaawaashko-bgoji-zhigaangwishiig zaasakokwangid
(Hot-green-wild-onions we fried.)

—all the energy of sun turned to leaf and ours to eat.
gwaashkweziwin aniibiishing teg, mii igo giizisan amwangid.
(The energy is in the leaves, so we are eating the sun.)

What a bear can eat, we can eat.
Mii i'iw miijinaa makwa, shkitoyaang miijinaamaang
(What a bear eats, we are able to eat.)

If, lost in the wilds,
Giishpin wanishinyaang gojing,
(If we are lost outdoors,)

we don't find a bear,
makwa gaawiin nandawaabamaasiiyangid
(if we don't find a bear,)

we can follow raccoon's paws printing a menu in mud
esibanan wii aanikeshkawangid ishkwa gii miijimikidowinan akiizhibiiaanan.
(a raccoon we're tracking after s/he wrote food words in the earth)

—nest eggs and berries, with minnows to finish.
wadiswaniwaawanoon miinwaa miinan miinwaa giigoozensag
(—nest eggs and berries and minnows.)

Or dig for our dinner in the dark
Miijim wii moonaamaang dibikong
(We'll dig for food in the night)

like raccoon going for grubs in stumps.
dibishko esiban moosegan moonawad giishkanakading
(like the raccoon looks for worms in a stump.)

Still, we cannot be sure of everything he eats.
Taa haa, kina gego da miijinaa gaawiin gikendaasiin
(Ah well, everything s/he eats we cannot know.)

We do not know every root,
Gaawiin nd'gikendaasiimin ensa ojiibik
(We don't know each root,)

cannot trust those people.
gaawiin debwetasiingidwaa gondag bimaadizijig.
(we cannot believe those people.)

Winter roots, round and pale cheeked,
Waawiyewaabshkaajiibikiigag
(Round white animate roots)

drawn through earth to the moon,
dibikigiizis zhaabonad aakiing
(by the moon are pulled through the earth)

heave up just enough to see the moon
miidash gimaabmaawad dibikigiizis
(then steal a peek at the moon.)

and say, softly so we can just hear:
gaaskanazowaad, epichii bizindawangid
(They whisper, while we listen to them:)

She is not our kind
Mayaganishinaabe aawed
(*She is a stranger,*)

—but how kind her face.
ah, minodengwe
(oh how nice her face,)

How far off and hungry her look.
Waasawaabam miinwaa chibakaded.
(she looks so far away and so hungry.)

II

Gizhi-ozhaawaashko-bgoji-zhigaangwishiig zaasakokwangid
        gwaashkweziwin aniibiishing teg, mii igo giizisan amwangid.
Mii i'iw miijinaa makwa, shkitoyaang miijinaamaang
Giishpin wanishinyaang gojing,
makwa gaawiin nandawaabamaasiiyangid
esibanan wii aanikeshkawangid ishkwa gii miijimikidowinan akiizhibiiaanan.
        wadiswaniwaawanoon miinwaa miinan miinwaa giigoozensag
Miijim wii moonaamaang dibikong
dibishko esiban moosegan moonawad giishkanakading
Taa haa, kina gego da miijinaa gaawiin gikendaasiin
Gaawiin nd'gikendaasiimin ensa ojiibik
gaawiin debwetasiiingidwaa gondag bimaadizijig.
Waawiyewaabshkaajiibikiigag
dibikigiizis zhaabonad aakiing
miidash gimaabmaawad dibikigiizis
gaaskanazowaad, epichii bizindawangid
        Mayaganishinaabe aawed
        ah, minodengwe
        Waasawaabam miinwaa chibakaded.

III

Hot-green-wild-onions we fried.
        The energy is in the leaves, so we are eating the sun.

What a bear eats, we are able to eat.
If we are lost outdoors,
if we don't find a bear,
a raccoon we're tracking after s/he wrote food words in the earth
        —nest eggs and berries and minnows.

We'll dig for food in the night
like the raccoon looks for worms in a stump.
Ah well, everything s/he eats we cannot know.
We don't know each root,
        we cannot believe those people.

Round white animate roots
by the moon are pulled through the earth
then steal a peek at the moon.
They whisper, while we listen to them:
        She is a stranger,
        oh how nice her face,
        she looks so far away and so hungry.

II
Prose Poems

Preeminent Gooseberry Bakwezhiigan

There once was a lad who loved pie. He had never made one before, but he'd eaten pie and had thought to himself, I can make better pie than the pie-makers, so he set out to make a pie.

He decided on a gooseberry pie, that (which) if he were to call it blueberry pie in Ojibwe, would get a big laugh. Whenever anyone said the word for blueberry pie in Ojibwe to non-Ojibwe speakers, that person got a big laugh because it seems like the longest word non-Ojibwe speakers have ever heard. And he knew it would be the non-Ojibwe speakers who would eat the pie so he decided to put the Ojibwe word for blueberry pie on the cover of the menu. Only he spelled it phonetically, rather than the popular double-vowel spelling. That way the Ojibwe readers would know that the menu was about baking pie for the Chimookiman, not for other Ojibwe, who might not buy it.

He never thought to consult a cookbook because, he figured, he had eaten pie and so he basically knew how to make one. First he mixed some flour and lard together, then he flattened it on the bottom of a pie tin, then he placed a bunch of gooseberries on top, then he crimped a second crust on top. Time proceeded in a blessedly orderly fashion as the pie heated in the oven. Then, when he imagined the pie was done, because it looked done and he had seen done, so it *was* done, he took it out of the oven. He offered this pie to the general public and because the public craved authentic blueberry pie, they ate it up.

They all seemed kinda pleased and amazed as they ate; although, some of them looked at the menu and thought, what pie is this? What are these lumps in the crust and why is it so sour, raw, and soggy? The Ojibwe women in the crowd might of (have) asked him if he had browned the bottom crust first, but they did not take the lad that seriously.

Everyone figured that someone who did not know the difference between raw gooseberries and cooked blueberries would not have known to make the piecrust in two steps. In short, most everyone judged him on his efforts to make pie rather than the resulting pie and never let on it was hard to swallow.

As they sampled their lukewarm gooseberries and pushed their crusts around their plates, they talked about Flaubert. They talked about Flaubert the way they never would talk about pie. They talked about Flaubert as if he told them something about the French, about parrots and about life. At the same time, because the human mind is capable of such work, some of them thought about French pastry and wished they were eating a pie of *Fruits De Boise Sauvages,* untamed wildberry berries, which would have been ever so much better because, well the French are better at all things pastry, just as the English are better at all things English, except maybe Nabokov. [Better at Nabokov?!!!]

Just as the lad accepted a smoke from a Turtle Mountain Michif (who offered it to him using the quite acceptable and customary "ciga swa"), the lad, because he was the authority, the author, the authenticator, realized that the narrative had gone deeply out of his control, had veered drastically toward metaphor, even poetry, and was verging on misplacing a modifier in a pale fire imitation of the variation in human speech/thought. Something had to be done. He uttered the word for blueberry pie in Ojibwe:

Miiniibashkimiinasigunbatagiingwesijiiganbiitooingwesijiiganibakwezhigan!

The assembled startled into laughter. Then the room fell into Silence, who was and is an Ojibwe and universal character whose story we all should all more often tell.

Mii'iw

In House

MANUSCRIPT TITLE: *Locomotive Signals*
#1) A poem series that fills out document headings. Commentary w/o humor or irony.
#2) Enhances various lists (Cultural, Diaspora, Gender) and offers a rare glimpse of urban life to educated young white people.
#3) Technique: bloodless/inkless white   space.
One controlled utterance that we used to call a long poem . . .
#4) Played out in dramatic bits and turns.
#5) Tone shifts for dramatic effect. Turns
ugly and sexual, unexpectedly.
#6) Composed of coherent sentences. Some play with line
breaks—lots of build up for the slightest, slightest moment of poetry.
Though serious and complex in subject, this book could be read in ten minutes.
The words just

           float

           off

the page

and blow by

           in wisps.

#7) This book would no doubt appeal to many, many listeners.
Perhaps readers would want to re-read it after hearing it?
#8) Teaching it takes about twenty minutes.
#9) The title *Locomotive Signals* never unloaded by this book-poem: Some loco. Some motive. No trains. No signals. No training or signaling. No.
#10) Would I buy this book? Maybe. Depends on if the artist were a former student, gone off to grad school and corrupted.
#11) Thus, even as I register my old fuddy-duddy complaints about the state of poetry (nice, complex old word-welded poetry),
#12) *I recommend this manuscript* as likely a good bet for the press.
#13) Minor edits needed. Revisit the gimmick of M-Fer-calling and blow-jobbery where pointless.

Dancer Origin Story

Some say she was born of Snow. I say no. Who her people were no one can tell, but for the mark in her look, the darkness, the heat in her bones shining through the gray day she was born. Was it in the morning? Or did she come in the night after cries and hurried movements of women?

Hours and hours it was forward and forward and then oblivious retreat. She paused and thought, she would not join us after all. Then waves sent her forward again and she pounded to be let through.

She came through the caul of that other world into ours beating through the body of a woman to be born and breathe. No matter how beyond she may seem, she shares with us that: Breath, our first movement and voice all at once.

March 1964. After that fact there's mystery, curious historical gaps. Possibilities.

She may be of the Whale People, the fishing folk who wandered inland long ago hauling with them their cooking pots made from whale skulls, on sleds of whale ribs—precious antiques from centuries lived on the waves.

It may be she was meant to leave her arboreal birthplace and go back to living on waves. For she's all ebb and flow, just as the sea shifts gray-green, blue-black, white-tipped, green again and then red in resigning sun or sun up.

Maybe Sea is her sister and looks after her, no matter how far she moves inland, beyond the smell of salt, amid the cliffs of glass and paths of asphalt.

Some call her by her work, that verb, dance. But hers is more an inhabitance. Being a being, animate verbs can do that, live within and make its own will, move your way of being in the world. We think we choose, but we are this: movement.

It is this Spirit that makes strangers wish her movements were theirs—watching her all unknowing she has already given them away. She is generous and bereft they say. It is the way of her folk, whomever they may be or were long ago.

Do you feel the translucent strength of that whale skin around you now, close to her?

Indigenous or spontaneous, a graced race surely birthed her. Or was she one of the Wild Man's young, born in the roar of waves to a lovely human maid stranded on an isle learning all she could from the shore who hushed:

Forward, retreat, forward, retreat,
scatter, splash, leap, forward, retreat,
retreat and forward once more
and more, ever once more.

Dancer in Twin Voices

Voice 1:	We were born attached—
Voice 2:	At the foot. My foot.
Voice 1:	My chest against her foot.
Voice 2:	Her heart dug around bones, toes, heel.
Voice 1:	She is always saying, whining sweetly:
Voice 2:	*Does it hurt, Dear Heart?*
Voice 1:	My tendons strung to her humming, her guitar twang.
Voice 2:	We cannot be separated, too dangerous—
Voice 1:	For me. She'd survive, thrive even.
Voice 2:	*It's a thin line . . .*
Voice 1:	Dear Heart always smiles and says:
Voice 2:	*There but for . . .* *There I go!*

Voice 1:   Besides, it's only my bloody, necessary muscle,
only my love—

Voice 2:   For you.
Her pulse pushes me up, propels me—

Voice 1:   Pulls her down.
You didn't think she did that alone?

Voice 2:   You notice the force that can't come from just one woman.
Up and breath stuck we hang a moment.

Voice 1:   Then she stomps me in the chest.

Voice 1 & 2:   Who doesn't have a twin like this?

Utopia Hawk

When she was in the second grade, Star Hawk's name was Stella Hawkins, I know because the teacher called on her with her whole name.

She had eyes like geodes and dressed like a mess.
Everyone knew her family lived on Old Man Crow's land in a tipi.
There hadn't been a tipi on the reservation in a hundred years, but there it was, as Grandma said:
>*Ripe with Hippies.*

Star Hawk told me her name was Star Hawk and that she hated when the teacher read her "government name" off the attendance roster. So, I called her Star Hawk, unless I got mad at her and then I called her Stella.

My grandma used to walk me to school. A mile on a windy, cold road. Star Hawk's folks dropped her at school in a rusty red pick up. She'd jump out of the truck bed and they'd just drive off.

She carried everything in a knit bag, a huge one: lunch, books, gym clothes, sneakers, everything in one big striped, homemade bag.

Sometimes Star Hawk looked sad, but it was hard to tell what was brimming in her enormous, crystalline, tetrahedron eyes. It was better not to look.

Who are your parents? I asked, because Indian kids asked that as a polite thing. Do you mean my Twins? She said.

Turns out Star Hawk had two sets of everything we would have in a family, two Moms and two Dads and each pair was called Twin.

She said they were looking for the Land of Milk and Honey.
I said:
>*Well I'm lactose intolerant and allergic to bees.*

For sure I never went home with her and when they left the reservation we all thought, well that was the oddest thing.

Old Man Crow said,
>*They asked and I offered and that is all we know of the story.*

My Fetal Beatles or an Embryonic Education in Commune

All I need is love and I get it all in hum and thunder.

The uterine walls of Star Hawk teach me not in telepathy, more like a white
board only of blood.

My season will be Mud, I'm told, just after Introspection Season. Once I am
born, I'll show in styles and stripes what I learned in utero.

But first I'll ask: Can we have cats? Do we pay taxes? Who does the dishes?
(I mean seriously who does the dishes? 'cause I heard some words about
the dishes . . .)

Until then, there's nothing to do, but learn how to be me
in time, inside,
but it ain't easy.

Indigenous Foods Allowed in Utopia

Not beef, not noodles. Not onion, not Smack Ramen. But manoomin—food that grows on water—and juneberries and walleye.

Not milk and not honey. But swamp tea, and mmmmm maple!

Red Vines: Lines for Deloria

Truck stop bucket offers red whips, miles worth of invert syrup—chew for the chaw-free, rich with red dye. In it for the long haul, we load up on licorice laces, punctuate our stories by bites placed in dramatic pauses.

RED is a flavor of its own, sweet imitation of nothing known in nature. Black whips, the ones we favor, seem extinct in truck stops. RED it is. RED for joy riding. GOD after all is RED and has been long before 1969, when Custer Died for Your Sins and the universe came alive and chokecherry trees became your relations.

Red vines for journey. Road trip with whips and sisters who whip me into shape, need it or not. We could skip the licorice ropes, do without or Double Dutch with them. In this bucket, there's enough red rope to string us all together, like relatives fed from the same rich vein.

We mistake what looks like a dead eagle for a dead eagle and turn a U to find it is a goose. But not before we swap Red Vines for tobacco, jump out on the shoulder. Poor goose. Who's to say we shouldn't honor you? Still we leave you, roadside, road-killed and toothsome to buzzards, our other relatives.

The road divides for a boat-shaped rest area.
There are five points to the Lakota Worldview.
Point one: The Universe is Alive.

Red berries near the rest stop attract us. We of the chokecherry. Women of the Chokecherry. We of the tree Deloria gives agency. Chokecherries choose us. Who doesn't know this?

Some berries listen. Some lead. For sure we know we find berries when berries want to be found.

Uncommon flavor, the chokecherry. Tastes like mouth: hot, red, sharp, dark. Sweetened now, most often, to a tolerable syrup. But on the road we like it red-black and tart. God is RED-dark, sharp—a mouth.

Snap the licorice, measure the miles in vines. Stay awake. Not for the flavor, for the snap. Pass some back. If only we could say what it is we taste . . . What is the flavor? Ineffability?

If the universe were alive, these vines would taste of chokecherry.

Taste of the fruit we picked at the rest stop, of the three yogurt cups we filled up, of the Auntie Tree with Agency. But none of us think that at the time. We just motor along snapping licorice and chatting.

She speaks her flavor through the air, the alive air of the universe and of the speeding vehicle, so we all say at once, hey,
RED VINES TASTE OF CHOKECHERRY.

Because suddenly, and ever after, they do.

III
Prose Originals

Quiet Cupboard

In a yellow-painted cupboard in the kitchen above the corn, bean, pea, tuna, and sardine cans, our family kept treasure. Oh, not real treasure. Except perhaps my German grandfather Louie's enormous red-gold ring, the size of a baby bracelet, in a brown jeweler's box below hooks hung with dozens of bronzed keys. There were a few watches hanging next to the aluminum flashlight with the red Morse code box, probably not gold watches. The key hooks looped up strings of baubles and glowing rosaries. For some time my mother's faux diamond, ruined by dish detergent, perched on the top shelf in a small, blue jeweler's box.

This yellow pantry, lined with mod-flowered contact paper in yolky tones, was also a naturalist's cabinet. Dusty jars of cocoons slung on twigs wintered there. A few specimen wild hickory nuts—we called *them pukons*, from the Ojibwe word—might have been stashed above the phone book and atlas. There were sometimes dried moths or water beetles next to wolf-head kerchief slides for Boy Scouts and rolled up 4-H ribbons. Once I opened this narrow room of mysteries to find an ivory blade of bone, a heron's skull grimacing mildly against a Green Stamp trading book.

Bones and berries and pods of scarlet runner bean. Boxes of bee comb wax and inner tube patch. Such collages greeted me if I peeked into the yellow cupboard. If no one was around, I could pick my way through pencil stubs to find the elusive white-leaded pencil that corrected serious mistakes. It was ringed with a thick band of tape and kept under adult control. The implication just now comes clear to me: Who knows what one of us might have erased with no tell-tale pink rubbings to alert our parents? What fact of our past might we have altered? What permission re-dated and re-given might have sent my siblings on adventure, given a pass from algebra or catechism?

In truth nothing much was restricted in our place, nor could it have been. Belongings flowed through our home in communal re-use. Private stores were rare with seven siblings and others occupying our American Foursquare. Only the few, delicate, natural items—petrified bison tooth, long white feather with a hard sharp quill, pressed four-leaf clover, stashed high in the yellow cupboard—were known to be hands off. And so the cupboard fell into accidental still life as detailed as any student painter would ever hope to arrange, but personal and ever-changing.

As rare as space was private time with a parent. One by one, our father took us hunting and what we hunted, it turned out, were the objects that might be enshrined in the yellow cabinet. The stated goal was to "get a deer," and so my father took his bow, and doe scent, and silver butane hand-warmers in blue flocked pouches. We set off into cold hours, very early or getting late, to walk along the Wildrice River. We each were given our turn to track deer, look for "evidence" of raccoon, find buck marking on trees, gather mushrooms, glimpse Pileated Woodpeckers, rare then, and enjoy how truly quiet we could be, moving between trees, along a cornfield, flat against a ditch, up a tree to perch while he went into the fields to try to flush a doe.

My father took me hunting only two or three times, but from those times I learned the skill of wait and watch. Was it hard, as it is for my own kids, for me to be quiet? I recall standing stick still. The trickle of water under a leaf-choked log roared as loud as a canyon river in those little woods. The red of those last dryland oaks, vivid when all else went gray, backgrounded the heart-shaped hoofprint filled with water, the mark of prey and the start of a brief race—the only sign of deer one day. These indications of more quiet lives, marked in hushed tones, pointed toward another way of being that comforted me even then. Life, even to a small girl in North Dakota, whirled with strife and uncertainty, but animals, birds, plants, rocks—they didn't worry about the world. They browsed, rutted, left scat, let their beauty be glimpsed, all in silence.

Except, of course, not all birds are quiet. My grandfather once called to say he heard cranes flying over his house on the reservation. Which direction? I asked. Honestly I thought the same birds might fly right down our street hundreds of miles away. Our parents engendered in us a common yearning, a family obsession to see the big birds: Great Blue Heron, Egrets, Pelicans, and the prize— Whooping Cranes. We hunted birds as much as deer, but without ill intent. This was the 1970s, just past the devastation of DDT, an uncertain time: were we saying goodbye to the last few large wading birds or seeing a return?

On country drives, Dad stopped the car and waited quietly when a flick of wading bird alerted us to watch the edge of a slough. And though I heard the resounding croak of cranes overhead, I've never for certain seen a Whooping Crane. The heron skull in the cupboard, we prized not just for its ivory beauty, but because it might be the last one, ever.

When I put my head in our yellow kitchen cupboard and tried a long smile, eye to empty socket, I could get back a little of the quiet I'd met out hunting with my father. I learned to carry that silence with me, to open a mental cabinet and sort a still life of bones, driftwood, foxtails, until I reached a place beyond everyday clamor, until I learned I could shut out what was just then rushing to my ears, the roar of the world in its everyday rage.

Two Sides

We live sweet and safe in our own home with two huge spruce trees watching over us. The phone rings and rings and we won't answer it because someone we love, someone with no home, keeps calling and calling. He speaks in perfect needs: I'm cold, I'm sleeping outside, I need money. We imagine his shy eyes, his sly white smile, the brilliant boy he was and it chokes us so that when we say no, it comes out a cough. Then we tell him we love him, ask him not to call anymore, and hang up.

In the mountains of Wyoming, between little cedars, we kids lived out of a tent one teenage summer. The boys slept like bears. Their snores so loud I'd stay awake fearful they would attract grizzlies. And I was cold, too cold to sleep. He rolled an arm around me, pulled his sleeping bag over us both. He bought a dozen eggs and boiled them so we would eat all week. He hauled the water. The phone rings and rings and he asks me every day this week for money. He's living in a park, the weather's changed, he can pay me back. I tell him, *Don't call again.*

Boys trampled through my girlhood in packs: brothers, cousins, Grandma's foster kids, relatives of one kind or another. Canine in their ways, they moved with the nod of the head or flick of the eyes. Wordlessly they knew to gather up fishing gear, crackers and canteens, and take off camping along the river. They were utterly free, it seemed to me, given leave by adults to adventure out, to fry up their own dinner, to keep out of trouble or face the music when the sheriff's car brought them home.

We bought this house two years ago and set to redeem it from its rental days. Still, windows cracked in parties past let in whistling drafts. The plumbing demands more immediate funding, so we'll plastic seal the glass another winter. The last hundred dollars we sent him, we meant to donate to Obama, a candidate who knows two sides of life. The split glass attracts my eye when the phone rings—but we wouldn't have fixed the window with that hundred anyhow. I let it ring and ring. My husband picks it up after a dozen calls. *Please don't call her again.* After that we get quiet, quiet, quiet, for almost a day.

Outside a trendy shop, my kids once met a man with cool high-tech prosthetics. His cardboard sign said IRAQ VET. With me, my kids get to choose to give and they do, every time—whatever change they have, or they ask me to loan them a dollar. They've seen me give cash all their lives. The tribal brothers

at the on-ramp, we hit with a fiver on payday. They are high as kites and proba-
bly violent bastards, but I just say, *Boozhoo*—greet them in our language—roll
down the window. I tell the kids we are two sides of the same life.

What we have means nothing. Nothing. There is no particular joy in giving.
And no guilt we might feed addiction. When he is high he forgets to call,
forgets our number sometimes. We've had years of quiet when he was in jail.
The phone does not ring and does not ring and does not ring until we do not
notice it not ringing.

Born a girl, I was flip side to the boys. They played in the dark. I came in when
the house lit up. American Indian men, born statistics, face a life of shortened
span, more likely to die violently or by accident. Three of my cousins dead
already—I will live their lives twice.

We do not need to remind ourselves those dozens of calls are nothing. They
are nothing. Nothing to our safe days and nights, sheltered under enormous
spruce, paying enormous taxes, playing our side of this one whole halved and
split, but same life.

Selected Work
(1997–2008)

from *National Monuments* (2008)

Guidelines for the Treatment of Sacred Objects

If the objects emit music,
and are made of clay or turtle shell,
bathe them in mud at rainy season.
Allow to dry, then brush clean
using only red cloth or newspaper.
Play musical objects from time to time.
Avoid stereotypical tom-tom beat
and under no circumstances dance or sway.

If objects were worn as funerary ornament,
admire them verbally from time to time.
Brass bells should be called *shiny*
rather than *pretty.* Shell ear spools
should be remarked upon as *handsome,*
but beads of all kinds can be told,
simply, that they are *lookin' good.*

Guidelines for the treatment of sacred objects
composed of wood, hair (human or otherwise),
and/or horn, include offering smoke,
water, pollen, cornmeal or, in some instances,
honey, chewing gum, tarpaper,
and tax incentives.

If an object's use is obscure,
or of pleasing avian verisimilitude,
place rocks from its place of origin
within its display case. Blue-ish rocks
often bring about discovery, black rocks
soothe or mute, while white rocks irritate mildly.
All rocks must return to their place of origin
whenever they wish. Use only volunteer rocks,
or stones left by matri-descendant patri-tribalists.

Guidelines for the treatment of sacred objects
that appear or disappear at will
or that appear larger in rearview mirrors,
include calling in spiritual leaders such as librarians,
wellness-circuit speakers and financial aide officers.

If an object calls for its mother,
boil water and immediately swaddle it.
If an object calls for other family members,
or calls collect after midnight, refer to tribally
specific guidelines. Reverse charges.

If objects appear to be human bone,
make certain to have all visitors stroke
or touch fingertips to all tibia, fibula,
and pelvis fragments. In the case of skulls,
call low into the ear or eyeholes, with words
lulling and kind.

If the bones seem to mock you
or if they vibrate or hiss,
make certain no mirrors hang nearby.
Never, at anytime, sing *Dem Bones.*

Avoid using bones as drumsticks
or paperweights, no matter
the actions of previous Directors or Vice
Directors of your institution.

If bones complain for weeks at a time,
roll about moaning, or leave chalky outlines,
return them instantly to their place of origin,
no questions asked. C.O.D.

Black and White Monument, Photo Circa 1977

I

Everything that ever happened
lies outside the white border
of this photo taken in the late 1970s.

Two girls holding babies in strong light with a field in the distance.

The girls' faces, obscured in deep shadows
on the left, show the high planes of their faces
in bright relief on the right. Not a good shot.

Not one to put in an album or mount in a frame or ever look at again.

We only knew each other those few hours
before and after the shutter snapped.

We hauled those babies, offspring of older cousins,
all over our Grandpa's land that one reunion weekend
and then never saw one another again.

Who were those babies? Which of our many cousins?
The girl in my arms, sweet-faced and prettily dressed—
probably belonged to my grown-up, glamorous cousin,
mother to three, already.

Our faces in half shade, strange above the babies' lit up scowls
and puffed out cheeks.

That cousin's baby, held against my relaxed arm,
my knee beneath her clutched in my right hand—
the only grown-up part of me. My long thighbones
slim for just that year, then rounded like the rest of me.

My pony legs and long wings of bangs above a shoulder-length fall
that match my cousin's and date the era.

Dark and light divide the shot. The light is off. The light is everything.

My grandparents' land stretches out beyond us, like the real subject of the photo.
The light on that land, beyond beautiful, went into me so young
it became the color of all yearning, all rest to be hoped for,
the face of heaven. Everything.

II

Dark slashed with too bright light. Two girls holding babies at sunset near a field.

Beyond the white border of the photo: a cabin of oak logs chinked with mud.
Old clothesline poles where swallows nest.
A burn barrel for trash. And one young tree,
a basswood wide enough to give deep shade to the drinkers,
meshed to lawn chairs—there for hours
before and after the photo.

They'll tall talk and fish iced beers from a galvanized tub.
When that ice melts, they'll fill it with iron-belt well water
that smells slightly of blood.

We drank from the pump in teams:
one cousin primes it, then cold, cold water gushes down the other's throat,
spills across the other's chest, so everyone walks away wet.

We will get up from that picture, hauling those babies.
We will get up on our long, adolescent legs
and move among the men who tease us for our baby love,
the sweaty infants clinging to our damp shirts,
our short shorts and snapping eyes do not stop their comments one bit.

Not a good shot. Not one I'd ever look at with that cousin saying:
"Look at us, we were so young . . ."

The boy baby wears little man clothes and plaid shoes tied up nicely.
He looks like he might head to the office, broker a deal, make a mint.
He looks like there's a plan for him. But *we know different,* as we said then.
We all *know different.*

Don't we always know more or less than what a photo can show?

The girls in that photo wear braces that make their lips puff up and part
when they mean to hold them stern, mean to avoid the eyes of men.

Not even a year later, they'll give in and want love
from any boy who drives them down dirt roads
bordered by sunflowers, hay, green corn.

III

Dark and light divide the shot. The light is off. The light is everything.

To think beyond the white border of that photo makes a click
                              deep in the cartilage that guards my heart.
It unfixes something in me where memory fights facts
                              about the half of us who have so little time.

Those beyond the border who would too soon die sick,
                              or senselessly, or go unrecognizable
in a life both dark then slashed with too bright light.

Why do we bear the cruelty of photos—the way they suggest anything
                              can stop, any moment can be saved?

Everything beyond that border comes along with that image
                              and then more images and more and more.

We got up, chased the toddlers until every beer was drunk
                              and every drunk passed out.
In the morning, we turned a hose on those sleeping it off under the basswood,
                              then hauled ass back to the cabin.

We found our Uncle working a hot pan of dredged and fried delicacies
from a yearling doe that Uncle shot leaning out his car window.

No one took his picture then or in the next moment when we sat down laughing
and ate the tender meats, the muscle that pumped her life,

                    the best, most vital parts of that deer.

Grand Portage

Here is the path my people walked
hauling immense trade canoes,
the semi-truck of centuries past.

Here between Great Lake and Great North,
earth curves visibly toward the arctic ice
that now flows in places never open before.

Here guests can hear a natural history
of the beaver, gold standard for
a century of trade from isle to inland.

Here re-enactments and regalia
keep history current, preserve trappers'
ways, traders' wares, all the era conveys.

Here ghostly silver warehouses of bare wood,
a portage path eight and a half miles:
full of meaning, necessary, contested.

Here a National Monument arose by
Presidential declaration to urgently protect
Gitche Onigaming's place in time.

Here begins North and territories beyond,
where ice opens a passage that, a century past,
would have made this path unnecessary, unprotected.

There the true path, the mark, the monumental.

Post-Barbarian

And now what shall become of us without any barbarians?
Those people were some kind of solution.
    —Constantine P. Cavafy, "Waiting for the Barbarians" (1904)

Such things as dazzled me,
emerald brilliance, glitter of
costly canes wonderfully carved
with silver and gold—mean nothing
now I've left the gates.
Left off my threats and treating,
ceased my distant drums and leaping
out at civil folk in dark barrens where my
young sleep piled like squirrels or dogs
or any creature you chose to call us.
Now what? Now who?
You draw a zone that attracts, holds terror
in its grasp, sticks flies in a paper trap.
Those bodies glitter, too, void, wrapped with yours,
litter the sand with metal husks and insect noise.
We see it on your televised maps and understand
fear of them keeps the vote in hand, solves
all economic woes, turns the key to homelessness,
best-guesses global warming,
antidotes AIDS, fixes inside fights,
unravels the mystery of misogyny,
tells the world: it's them-not-me.

So, we know what has become of you, who needed us,
your *kind of solution.* But what was it we once solved?
What was the quandary? Who asked the question?

Some Elsie

And there she sits, Elsie, in American Lit.,
at the Community College or Harvard or the U.
The sleek New York TA reads how her family
"married with a dash of Indian Blood"
and thus escaped the fate of the "pure products"
Wm. Carlos Wms. saw go crazy.

Does she sit, terrified or transfixed?
Waiting for someone to turn, look at her and think,
There she is, that Elsie.
So what if she was hemmed all around with murder?
Or if a few of her relatives had screws loose?
She'd deny bathing in filth from Friday to Sunday.
What a girl does on the weekend,
come on now, that's her own affair.

She endures the comments about her body,
"the great ungainly hips and flopping breasts."
What if her ample chest had been her pride?
What if, at first, she flushed at the sound of
"voluptuous water" and took it as a compliment?

What if, at first she thought, *Ah, at last
a poem about someone I know.*
Imagining that she'd strain after deer, too,
if stuck in the suburbs passing pills.
But now, even knowing her hips,
somehow become, the TA says, *a text,*
doesn't help the sting when she thinks
there's some truth she'd like to express,
broken brain or not.

In Search of Jane's Grave

In memory of Jane, wife of Henry R. Schoolcraft, Esq., born at St. Mary's Falls, 1800;
died at Dundas, May 22nd, 1842, in the arms of her sister, during a visit at the house
of the rector of this church, while her husband was in England and her children at a dis-
tant school. She was the eldest daughter of John Johnston, Esq., and Susan, daughter of
Waubojeeg, a celebrated war chief and civil ruler of the Odjibwa Tribe.

—INSCRIPTION AT JANE JOHNSTON SCHOOLCRAFT'S GRAVE

Woman of the Sound the Stars Make Rushing through the Sky,
Bamewawagezhikaquay, her headstone should have said.
But her name splits, eclipsed by his,
her co-author and husband.
Jane, wife of, it reads,
followed by a sonnet,
tightly rhymed to fit lines
together to say she died *bland*
and sure of immortality:
She smiled to quit a world of tears.

If only the words left us were hers.
Literary Grandmother,
first Ojibwe, mixed-blood,
Native, First Nations, Indian writer.
Mother poetess.

True, her verse hurts like 1830.
She kept current, do not doubt it,
wrote no worse than Longfellow,
who took her mother's family stories
(as offered by her husband, Schoolcraft)
and Hiawatha-ed the heck out of them.

In a small town cemetery, I thought
I'd found you, our literary Sky Woman.
Someone re-created your grave,

The sonnet at least, minus your name,
but nearer to your girlhood home
where you were known and loved as
Woman of the Sound the Heavens Make.

Dear Jane, hushing pines along the lake
should have sung you rest eternally—
peaceful on the point, Michigan
beating blue and flecked,
rushing like stars to the shore.

The Theft Outright
After Frost

We were the land's before we were.

Or the land was ours before you were a land.
Or this land was our land, it was not your land.

We were the land before we were people,
loamy roamers rising, so the stories go,
or formed of clay, spit into with breath reeking soul—

What's America, but the legend of Rock 'n' Roll?

Red rocks, blood clots bearing boys, blood sands
swimming being from women's hands, we originate,
originally, spontaneous as hemorrhage.

Un-possessing of what we still are possessed by,
possessed by what we now no more possess.

We were the land before we were people,
dreamy sunbeams where sun don't shine, so the stories go,
or pulled up a hole, clawing past ants and roots—

Dineh in documentaries scoff DNA evidence off.
They landed late, but canyons spoke them home.
Nomadic Turkish horse tribes they don't know.

What's America, but the legend of Stop 'n' Go?

Could be cousins, left on the land bridge,
contrary to popular belief, that was a two-way toll.
In any case we'd claim them, give them someplace to stay.

Such as we were we gave most things outright
(the deed of the theft was many deeds and leases and claim stakes
and tenure disputes and moved plat markers stolen still today . . .)

We were the land before we were a people,
earthdivers, her darling mudpuppies, so the stories go,
or emerging, fully forming from flesh of earth—

The land, not the least vaguely, realizing in all four directions,
still storied, art-filled, fully enhanced.
Such as she is, such as she wills us to become.

Elsie Drops Off the Dry Cleaning

What's this in his pocket? A prescription pad.
If only she were bad, she'd write some 'ludes,
but instead she thinks to pen a few lines,
like the master himself, confine her desires
to the square under his name and Rx.

In the time it takes the rack to rotate,
her order's in, starch the white coats,
press the slacks for pick up in two days.
Meanwhile her mind's a hummingbird,
flits words to square, then darts away.
She needs more room, more lines.

Next store over's office supplies:
Big Chief tablets thick with lines,
the pulpy paper almost moist, acrid,
so soft pencil rips it. She buys crayon instead.

This is how Elsie winds up in American Lit.
First her words on Big Chief then, in years,
Son of Big Chief tablets appear. Her career
as a house-girl is long over. She hitchhikes:

Oklahoma, Colorado, South Dakota, takes lovers.
But her braids-n-shades warrior, without feathers,
whose beads and groovy vest protect her words,
does more for her than one man ever could.

Son of Big, as renewable as wood, dependable.
Tablets get her through the '70s drug-free,
nearly sober, raising kids and hell for AIM.
Then one day she enrolls in college, reads.

And writes, and writes, straddles a canon, makes a name.

Butter Maiden and Maize Girl Survive Death Leap

Even now, Native American Barbie gets only so many roles:
Indian Princess, Pocahontas, or, in these parts, Winona—
maiden who leapt for brave love from the rock where eagles mate.

In my day, she might have played Minnehaha, laughing waters,
or the lovely one in the corn oil ads: "We call it maize . . ."
Or even Captain Hook's strangely erotic Tiger Lily.

Oh, what I would have done for a Chippewa Barbie.
My mother refused to buy tourist souvenir princesses
in brown felt dresses belted with beads, stamped Made in China.

"They're stunted," Mom would say. Her lips in that line
that meant she'd said the last word. She was right, those dolls
were stubby as toddlers, though they wore women's clothes.

Most confusing was the feather that sprouted at the crown
of each doll's braided hair. "Do they grow there?"
a playmate once asked, showing me her doll from Mount Rushmore.

I recall she gazed at my own brown locks then stated,
"Your mother was an Indian Princess." My denial came in an instant.
My mother had warned me: "Tell them that our tribe didn't have any royalty."

But there was a problem of believability, you see, a crumb of fact
in the fantasy. Turns out, Mom had floated in the town parade
in feathers, raven wig and braids, when crowned the college "Maiden."

Her escort was the college "Brave" they chose each autumn.
Oh, Mom . . . you made it hard on us, what you did at 18—
and worse, the local rumor that it was *you* on the butter box!

You on their toast each morning, you the object of the joke,
the trick boys learned of folding the fawn-like Butter Maiden's
naked knees up to her chest to make a pair of breasts!

I cannot count the times I argued for Mom's humble status.
How many times I insisted she was no princess, though a beauty
who just happened to have played along in woodland drag one day.

I wonder, did my sisters have to answer for the princess? Did you?
Couldn't we all have used a real doll, a round, brown, or freckled,
jeans and shawl-wearing pow-wow teen queen? A lifelike Native Barbie—
better yet, two who take the plunge off lover's leap in tandem and survive.

The Lone Reader and Tonchee Fistfight in Pages

Have I not been your faithful sidekick?
Have I not been your faithful Indian guide?
Have I been, at least, your Sacajawea,
hankering for her mother tongue, slogging,
baby on the back and all? Your insider
reading the trail, trailing the readings
so as to point a way? Forgive me,
Kein No Sabe. You know not what
you know not, I know.
I do not mean to keep from you
tribal secrets, tribal sec-texts,
secret tribes or textual innuendo.
Only, my tongue refuses to fork, fork you
off into the path not-to-be-taken—
for that has made all our differences.

Full Bodied Semi-Sestina

We take on pounds, heavy as cast iron,
we increase. We grow substantial, fat
even, and luxurious, although we tire
easily, puff in effort, purr and doze. We join
weight loss groups and confess and lift
up wafers of diet bread, punish our tongues.

What good is the human tongue
if it cannot lap molasses rich with iron,
fortification against poor blood? What a lift
we get from a little dab, some mono-fat,
mayo, or other loveliness. Won't you join
us in our lust, our great inflation of the spare tire?

It is not just about what we crave or that we easily tire
of ordinary fare. It's just we've lit the tongue
on fire. An urgent flame that leaps the join
between brain and body, makes food knowledge, iron-hard
fact to be visited, an experience. In command, Fat,
takes on her own life, though she's our burden to lift.

Or it may be she's simply unfit, no matter if fashion lifts
restrictive notions of where women can jiggle. Fad may tire
of the diamond between the thighs, impossible for body fat
in the normal range, not to mention genetics, the iron-clad
code we obey without knowing. A grandfather's love of tongue
sandwiches and sausage and schnapps is a club you join

just by being born. How simple is it to un-join?
How much must you want to lift
your own children from the shackles, the iron
set to weigh them down? Who wouldn't tire
with so much to bear? What prayer can we tongue
to deliver us all from fat?

It is not even that we hate our fat.
We love ourselves. We who join
the matrimony of flesh. To hold our tongues
begins a long divorce. Forks un-lift,
we deflate like a blown tire,
shouldered off-road tire-iron

in hand to beat the fat. *Iron
will!* Too tired a chorus to join,
yet we lift our tongues.

Body Works

She labors. She efforts.
Raw as mutton, she functions.
Beloved body. Never leave me.

Never lend museums
your tissues, triceps, glutes.
Do not expose your inner works

as some corpse did,
in a busy airport
where a gray curtain gap

showed me jerked
and plasticized muscle
as my walkway glided past.

Work, just work.
Grin a death's head beneath
my plump and living cheeks,

but never leave me, body.
I will not make you art.

Even now she pumps, spasms,
pulps my dinner within her.
She works. Her blue fluids

meaningless and messy
illustrate nothing of her fine
compunction, her systole

and distally. She does it all
free and out of love for me.
Or so it seems.

She works. She labors.
My children, made in her,
came waxy and bloody enough.

Why would I want to know
any other innards than hers?
What intimacy has she spared

that I'd find splayed,
preserved and presented
upon a platform with expert didactics.

Work, just work. Make love.
What better act could she
perform in plastic?

Never leave me, body.
Though there's just one of me
and uncounted insatiable others

lined up to get a look
at what I take for granted:
guts, gonads, gallbladder,

your brilliant splash and gulp
hot hemoglobin,
vibrant hum of human synapse,

electricity that, if we listen
closely sings in any body.
Any body, believe me.

Bodies work.
We're proof enough.
Or we should be.

Kennewick Man Tells All

We didn't go digging for this man. He fell out—he was actually a volunteer. I think it would be wrong to stick him back in the ground without waiting to hear the story he has to tell.

—FORENSIC ANTHROPOLOGIST JAMES CHATTERS, DESCRIBING
KENNEWICK MAN IN THE *NEW YORKER*, JUNE 16, 1997

Ladies and Gentleman of the press—

Kennewick Man will now make a brief statement
after which he will answer questions as time permits.

I am 9,200 years old.

I am bone. I am alone.

Kennewick Man Attempts Cyber-date

And then, one evening, I turned on the TV and there was Patrick Stewart—Captain
Picard of Star Trek, *and I said, "My God, there he is! Kennewick Man!"*

—FORENSIC ANTHROPOLOGIST JAMES CHATTERS
IN THE *NEW YORKER*, JUNE 16, 1997

So when Cyber-date asks me what I look like,
I'm no liar.

Not like I expect to match a hottie.
Not looking for "Barbie and Kennewick Man"—

But to smell a woman's neck again!

Or just fill all required fields.
To simply state:
My age,
My race,
My God.

Kennewick Man Swims Laps

For more than 40 years, the bones of about 12,000 Native Americans have been kept in drawers and cabinets under the swimming pool of the Hearst Gymnasium, next door to the museum.

—"Berkeley Accused of Racism over Failure to Return Tribal Bones," *Los Angeles Times*, February 27, 2008

Aquamarine with navy lines to keep
me in my lane. Lap, lap, lap,
again and again until I hear
their watery voices beneath
repeating all I said when dead:

Peace, peace, peace and sleep.

A few cry out: *Remember me!*
But I am older than religion,
and remember only river talk.

Lap, lap, lap, then turn in aqua *agua*.
I'm used to water, lay dead along
a river's edge nine millennia.

But water here's unnatural, vivid.
Still, I am older than religion,
—gotta keep limber. Lap, lap.

Aqua's such an off color,
new to me like rubber, milk,
electricity, and jealousy.

Tribes and pre-Christian Folk groups
claim my water-logged bones as their own.
So too, the dead under lane seven. Lap.

May Day the Morris Dancers, subversive
at sunrise along chilly urban riverbanks,
shake bells and batons and ribbon bands . . .

Perhaps my kind?
Lap. Turn.
There is no mine.

I am older than any name for God,
swimming in the voices of blue-green ghosts,
in a place where color speaks

the way pool water changes shades,
renames itself with every ripple, every wave.

Prisoner No. 280

The Widow Capet,
buried in a mass grave,
quicklimed with her kind
and ignoble others, found
anonymity until her garter
gave her remains away
and they dug her up,
placed her by her husband's side
in the crypt for royal tenants.

There St. Denis stands with mitered head
in hand, his halo still aglow above
his raggedly chopped neck.

Saints before the time of guillotine
bore less scientific execution,
endured rough decapitations, yet walked,
some for miles. Their sermons they gave
to the last, to the grave made on the spot
where their bodies finally dropped.

Basilicas sprang up where such saints stopped,
churches fit for kings, their widows, and orphans,
who may have lost their heads, but none their hearts
—customarily embalmed as souvenir.

Prisoner No. 280 had given birth in public,
so execution merely brushed her dignity—
her last words a *pardon moi* as she tread
the executioner's boot.

The final words she left her boy asked
he not avenge her death. He lived eight years,
most in prison torture, forced drunkenness,
t.b., then death found the Lost Dauphin.

She would have died to save him,
and tried, when the military arrived to pry
the child from his mother. That's what it took.

His heart did survive, not embalmed,
but bottled by the surgeon in alcohol
until the days of testing DNA—
Marie's own mother mitochondria
identified the boy's heart as of the royal line.

In the year of her Lord, 2004,
they put that pickled organ to rest
with all the rest of the royals at St. Denis,
guarded by the headless patron of headache,
to whom we might now pray with all our hearts.

Vial

Recently, contact with the outside world has brought the Karitiana access to the Internet, where they discovered that their blood and DNA samples are being sold online.

— LALO DE ALMEIDA FOR THE *NEW YORK TIMES*

Tube of red
like a lipstick,
passion's paint,
paid for yet
unpaid for,
filched like a drugstore
compact pinched.

Glass finger
slender vial of DNA
For Sale
to non-profits
yet non-bought
non-paid for.

Promised medicine,
Karitiana, Amazonian
indigenous, offered
blood and got
nothing.

Rich and red
blood of hunger
bled in fear of

the next world wanting
the body whole,
each drop accounted for. . . .

When they sell it all,
they'll come back
for more.

Girl of Lightning

The bodies seemed so much like sleeping children that working with them felt "almost more like a kidnapping than archaeological work," Dr. Miremont said.
—New York Times, September 11, 2007

Thunder loves you,
mumbles charms to warm
you—folded cold body.

Lightning's pity picks you,
licks a kiss, but what's left
to wick?

Even direct hits miss—
no amount of flash and hiss
fires you. Inviolate virgin,

inflammable channel to Gods
long gone or gone underground,
ghost-gray flecks left in the rock

altar, your shelter for five centuries
where you huddled, red-painted
hair and wreathed with feathers.

Weave threads of your shawl—
not a shroud since you were live
when left for dead—weave cover

please, I beg your handlers.
Pull stitches so that wound closes
over your smoldered remains.

They say you clutch your mother's hair,
strands in a bag sent up the mountain,
an introduction to the Gods

of Science, who read threaded
DNA to determine who you
were related to when human.

Not the crushed boy near you,
no brother he nor sister the girl,
bound away to sacred silence,

cased in plastic cased in glass.
Visitors point and justify the past:
See what they did—child sacrifice.

Fattened 'em up, drugged 'em—
Spanish violence, Christian influence,
border fences, all deserved because of her

wad of coca leaves and elaborate braids.
Lightning's mark spares you display.
Singed cheek and blasted chest,

blackened flesh looks less asleep,
flashes back the fact you're dead,
a charred mummy, so far gone even

Lightning's longing couldn't wake you.
Thunder won't forget you, hums
a generator's song in cooler vents

to your coiled form in cold storage—
song of your six years plus five centuries
come to this: doom, doom, doom.

Lightning still sighs: *release, release, release.*

from *The Mother's Tongue* (2005)

Offering: Words

Gichimookomaanimo: speaks American, speaks the Long Knives' language

Mother, if you look it up, is *source*,
(fount and fountainhead—origin,
provenance and provenience,
root) and *wellspring*.
Near her in the dictionary you will find
we all spring *mother-naked*,
(bare, stripped, unclothed, undressed, and raw)
with nothing but *mother-wit*
(brains, brain-power, sense) our *native wit*
with which we someday might *mother*,
(nurse, care for, serve, and wait on)
if we don't first look it up and discover
the fullness of its meaning.

Such interesting language, this *tongue*,
(our diction, idiom, speech, and vernacular)
also *sign language*,
(gesture language)
and *contact language*,
which was English or Ojibwe,
either way; both spoke forward our *mother country*,
our *motherland* (see also fatherland,
our home, our homeland, our land)
called *soil* in English our *mother tongue*,
our *native language* that is not my *Native language*
not the *mother language* Ojibwe:
wellspring of many tongues, nurse, origin, and source.

She Dances

The drum begins and she
raises her hand to lift
the female-feathered fan.
She moves slowly, heavy
in her buckskin, heavy
with the possibility of life.
Her neat fringe beats along
with the drum as she steps.
Full sun in full leather and
she wills herself not to sweat.
I pray the long days in the arena,
nights sleeping on the ground,
make her ready to dance labor.

Though it's my right, I never dance.
Not in a shawl, with fluid moving fringes,
not with beads offered up leggings,
no satin-worked ribbons or cones sewn
in V-shapes have ever drawn an arrow down
my hips to point the way to being woman.

But I once dreamed my friend a dress:
one in slipping honey colors of satin
with black bands. Its music came with,
its cones jangling and flashing near each
flower-print cloth outfit then on to the next.
And now I dream her another dress,
the one for labor, a traditional deep blue,
the midnight wool blue shot with red
that all her ancestors would recognize,
the heavy dress of history,
the one made of flags
and ration blankets and blood.

Stung

She couldn't help but sting my finger,
clinging a moment before I flung her
to the ground. Her gold is true, not the trick
evening light plays on my roses.
She curls into herself, stinger twitching
gilt wings folded. Her whole life just a few weeks,
and my pain subsided in a moment.
In the cold, she hardly had her wits to buzz.
No warning from either of us:
she sleeping in the richness of those petals,
then the hand, my hand, cupping the bloom
in devastating force, crushing the petals for the scent.
And she mortally threatened, wholly unaware
that I do this daily, alone with the gold last light,
in what seems to me an act of love.

This Body, The River

After a painting by Jim Denomie, Asiginak

Phthalo:

        All that time I ran underground, green as mud.
        I didn't know I would flow until
        some boy stretched out with me by the river—

Cadmium:

        stretched me to my water self,
        my still but moving center
        that entered me in the spring
        still cool enough for breath to come
        in clouds and me so young I thought it was love

Ultramarine:

        to be so close to the dark movement of water
        in the hard bed, through frozen riverbanks
        bristling with new grass and just that once

Titanium:

        just that first time, this body, the river
        flows around stones, whorls an undertow,
        makes a map, borders another territory,
        divides up the whole wide wet world.

The Deep

Sparrows up the column of the maple
make a god-awful racket first thing,
first light, ever since April. The little twerps
are easy to read: I need, I need!

The adults, hysteric with lusty pride,
simply shriek and shriek without message.
They wake the newly pregnant woman
who cannot at first identify her feeling,

but remembers another dawn, an outing
by sea to watch for whales. Who ever honestly
expects to see creatures so ancient, so huge?
Now she rides the same unexpected waves

of sickness in unstoppable rhythm, in swells
that tossed her hanging, wretched at the rail.
No one else saw the great humpback whale
who eyed her, alone there at the back of the boat.

The birds' persistent racket, the jets at takeoff,
sound to her ill brain like doom. She blocks it all,
hangs on her emblem of belief: the rolling water,
the great being revealed, real, watching her from the deep.

Craving, First Month

My belly rejected everything but a certain sky,
the one that rocks the high north plains of home.
Nothing but color and light for my mouth,
streaks of cirrus like pale lettuce—tear a leaf
and taste that clear covering of clouds!
I craved the prairie. Wild as Rapunzel's mother,
I would have paid the witch's price,
but my dear sister agreed to drive
into the horizon, north and north for hours,
the car skimming along the two-lane blacktop
between acres of flooded field. We were asea
in the land that bred us. It fed us and we were happy.
The rush of passing color like fuel—
waves of chartreuse—mustard weed lapping the ditches,
confusing waves of sky grown on earth—flax blue as mirage.
Then a doe, then her blazing fawn springing ahead of us
red against the new crown of hard winter wheat.

That's what I grew my son on, month one.
I went hungry into the flat north
toward the reservation.
I ate it all.
Even the dusty green of the little-leaf sage
that covers my grandparents' grave
tasted good in my eyes.
Here it is, I said into wind up the bald hill.
Here it is, I said to the question mark of child.
Here's the land we are born from. Here's what made us.
Here's the world that fed us. Here now, you eat too.

Offering: The Child

We need a salt lick
to draw the deer-child,
the wild soul hovering
at the fringes of our existence.
We need to ask it home.

Or if we had a photo to post
like the ones we see at rest stops
that tell the world this one is wanted—
Come Home.

How to know what to offer,
what life it is that we offer?

We have nothing to lure
a whole new being
out of the tree edge of the future,
across the snow sweep of days
into the ring of our lives.

Finally we offer what our own fathers gave:
Names of ferns and birds,
the Purple Martin house posted each year
so now blue wings mean hope to us both.

We offer the wild rides with our mothers:
dented fenders, cars forgotten in the lot,
the Neapolitan melted on the dash.

In the end, we ask it as a favor:
Child, return us to days we thought were past.
Bring our grandmothers at the clothesline with you.
Bring our grandfathers in denim coveralls back.

We will all go berry-picking more often.
We'll do it right this time.

Kookum

Did she watch to morning? Tend the stove's fire,
her tiny infant boy nested in a shoe box, a crate
just his length that would do for a coffin, if she had to.

Was he like a boy from a story? So small he fit in a shoe,
slipped in with a wrapped and heated brick to incubate
this son who would be father of my own mother,

my grandfather whose Ojibwe words the wood's
edge heard daily and I heard too, rarely, mornings
when he bent, I now know, to offer pipe and prayer.

Did she fill the copper kettle? Kindle the fire
by her boy child, another of thirteen—the seventh,
and this one bound to lead his people, given Moses
as his second name—meant for politics and all of us.

Did she pray the rosary in vigil? Or call for Shyoosh,
her husband's sister who helped her deliver cures,
who delivered babies by the hundreds over many years.

Like sisters in a myth, did they sit up? Keep the child alive,
get him baptized, then take the buggy, ride to Canada
to ask for the same Indian Doctor, the Mashkiki Innni,
who later treated the mystery of great-grandmother's fits.

Did they manage it alone? Two women always proud to tell,
the story goes, how they warmed the tiny babies with a brick,
a box, and kept them breathing steam off of wet cloth.

We tell it now and you tell it later. Women will do as they must.
Or else none of us and less of them and not this story,
but the one with fewer questions and a far more certain end.

First Rice

For Jim Northrup

The grains should be green as river rocks,
long as hayseed, with the scent of duckweed
and sweetgrass that grows along the lake's banks.
First *manoomin*, feast plate laid for the spirits—
berries and tobacco offered with song.
What it must have meant to give
what little the people had to give:
herbs left in thanks for the food that will sustain us,
for the water that gives up that food,
for the world working the way it should
—living and full of living god.

What Pregnant Is Like

You get bigger.
I mean you enlarge,
diffuse, push boundaries,
cover the whole of woman,
man, and child. You balloon,
stretch in unexpected directions,
expand to contain whole lives with your
lone body. Your body becomes an extension,
a shelter built of love that takes the man in again
and again to hold all three inside. Such a good place,
such a good planet, so heavy you make your own gravity.

Young Poets with Roman Noses

The man beside me on the bench outside my college library
was the poet Milosz, but I did not yet know it,

as I admired his brambled eyebrows, his steady hand on the cup
while my own shook with nicotine and afternoon tea.

I was shy and unstudious, only out to glimpse young poets
with sharp features and perfect diction. There were a few,

and two of those would speak to me: One slight as a dancer,
the other muscled like a superhero sketch, all with lovely, lovely syntax.

I watched for them, came daily to free tea and did not know
Milosz sat beside me. When we spoke it was of the trees, the tea,

never poetry, bless him. That would have been beyond me.
I was expert only at love and thought I might love a poet-boy

if he would have me. I picked a bearded one from a distance whose nose
I described to my journal as roman, but not knowing what that meant

made my way past him to the OED. Oh, rich proximity!
He was there next to me. I forget what the dictionary told,

or what I might later have composed on the bench, although
twisting trees, red brick taken by ivy, lamps' rich pools on leatherette

were likely subjects in that time. I followed the poet boys to class,
found out the stature of my bench mate, never loved a one of them.

But how my fate clicked in those moments! Looking at noses,
wondering if they were roman, becoming poet by osmosis.

Years later a gentle listener came to hear me read and after
took my hand. His plan to marry a poet worked out better

than my own. And so I'd like to thank them, those young poets,
reach them—They led me to my life and love. Maybe they'll read

these lines and write, care of the editor. Maybe they will know
I'm grateful, I love my life. My life because of them, because of them

my love.

Another Touch

We hold hands in a Minnesota movie house
in midwinter, the air a tropical fog of breath
left by matinee patrons before we sat down.
I turn my palm up in yours. An *oven* in my
last month, I would prefer the other picture:
cold murder done in manufactured snow
an hour north of here. But tension makes
the baby jump, so it's steamy Elizabethans
filling the screen with endless undressing.
The film's good, but my hand's as restless
as the hero's whose love is constantly undone
in hoops and laces and collars. My hand flips
over and over in the heat of yours, won't give up
this gesture, knowing how soon our touch
will be translated for the one we made of it.
The lovers on the screen are still undressing—
all those stays and jerkins and then, *good god,*
an excruciating unbinding. My hand rolls in yours
seeking to be warmed and cooled at once,
to be naked and covered at once. That touch
we've shared so long will soon give birth
to another kind of touch: kin to the passion
we've rocked out of our bodies all these years,
but played out in tender strokes to the one
who just now rolls across the walls of me to drub
its own small fists against what it cannot know as other,
what is still me, touched by you, not yet three.

Nesting Dolls

I've been golden in the long afterglow,
I've been that bubble in the honey pot,
I've been sweet, sweet in me
and all along someone else.
That's the mystery.
First the man gives up his driblet of will,
it leaves his body to enter mine and in a moment
start another body that will leave mine.
It's what we all crave and sense; the memory
of such harmony, then a series of losses, separations.
The egg, the gold bubble in me, once in my Ojibwe mother,
once in her Ojibwe mother, and so on back
like nesting dolls. Now we tip the jar,
watch the slow pour of gold, the bubble thins,
grows toward self, toward that lovely love of self.

Craving Release

Evening primrose should egg the labor on.
Or it could make your body yawn and yawn
without real sleep for a week.

How can a whole person
grow at once so large
and stay as thin as tension
that holds water in a drop?
As curved as the edge of resistance,
bent to the point we break from self
into other selves.

This cannot happen, but it does.
Women blown full to shimmering,
inside attracted to outside,
whole, then parts, then parted.

We've been in bed forever with this lover
who has kept us on the brink of pleasure
until it's torture. Oh, let's just get it over.

Sisters Stay On the Other Side

Sisters there flows a river, dark green
or golden spring or a muddy channel
where we drown to the sound of lullabies.

Sisters stay dry on the banks, do not even
touch toe to test the water. Stop your ears
when you hear siren sounds: wet, sweet wails
that insist you can never understand
life, love, woman, man—until you birth
or nurse or raise a child in this world.

Sisters stop your ears, ignore our voices,
garbled, gargled in the milk-stream:
You do not need these things to live,
though there is a life you will not live,
worlds wet with another atmosphere
you'll never breathe, yet still you breathe.

Sisters, stay on the other side, stay dry.
Someone must read in a pool of lamplight.
Someone must rise from the favorite chair.
Someone must leave books eased open.
Someone must hum to herself, pour wine,
hear only her own ear, un-tuned to our wet cries.

New Born

In the beginning
we had to say your name
to get you to stay.

Your body twisted in motions
practiced in the womb.
We tried to see the grace

you would have had in water.
Only your long hands swaying, gestured
something lovely. But oh, those constant

tortured jerks and spasms—as if you were not
quite in your body yet, but struggling in
as though into a too tight suit!

Even your eyes, your alien,
hematite eyes, when open in rare times,
seemed to belong to a creature only.

There was no human spark, just flickers, then dark.
We had to say and say your name, chant it,
call you into your body—

inhospitable though it seemed with its blood
bright in the skin, too hot or cold. Bouts of rage
left you shaking like a pup. And the hunger

that stabbed you every hour. Pitiful.
Why would you have wanted to stay,
if we hadn't said and said your name?

Where were you when we called?
A long echoing way off or near
as we sensed, tethered to the body

in an envelope so thin and shiny,
so hard and curved and reflective,
we could not see?

In the beginning we had to choose,
grab a line of words, find a name
that would call you from that place.

We said it and finally your eyes lit.
Your cord stump darkened and fell.
We sewed it into a pouch, a beaded turtle

whose legs point in the sacred four directions,
whose back holds up the world—this world
you now claim with your radiant, human gaze.

Offering: Ojibwe

Some leaf taps the classroom window.
I am wondering what's the Ojibwe word for poem,
while my teacher says, *There is a spirit*
who helps the language live.
We should make offerings to that alive
spirit and ask for help.
Then he gives the quiz.
I bomb it because the words leap live
from the page to the open window
where the spirit catches them, quizzes:
Was it the one who was trying to write a poem?
Tell her to open the window and drift an offering down.

Sometime before the end of this poem
I go outside, try to ask that spirit,
who's got its job cut out, for help.
I think: *I do not have the right, the right words.*
And back beside my window: *I only have my poems.*
Then words drift, offering in their own right their own life.

Craving: Bitter Root

What I know of home—
tanned bed of dry, tall grass,
hot scent in August sun,
sweet oils baked by days
long as the globe of sound
surrounding us from a million wings
creatures strum to the sun, the sun,
the low-hung northern sun.
What I know of home—
car hung up on a rock,
out of the bush three brothers
walk, help carry the car off.
We drive and drive, drink the road.
What I know of home—
tastes sometimes like medicine,
take it in and let it out,
bitter root, *wi'sugidji'bik,*
the Indian physic that should cure all.
What I know of home—
nothing, nothing that won't heal.

Twin Bugs

Creamy tan, pinstriped in maroon,
custom Volkswagens cut me off
in mid–joy ride. This must be a dream
because I hate the highway.
But speeding along toward the skyline,
the IDS and all the high-rises big as life,
bigger and more lifelike, almost landscape,
now I love the road and am delighted,
when I should be enraged to see
two driver-less twin bugs cut in front
from either side. Two green vanity plates read:
Waabaabigan,
Wajiw gete.
The people's car, convertibles, deep red interiors
in cushy leather, write down my lane:
White clay,
Mountain of old times, or
Mountain of history.
Two mysteries I translate imperfectly,
twin Ojibwe words that now also mean
to wake laughing from a dream
that leaps language from the chest.

Vermillion Hands Petroglyph

Red ochre on rock, this kiss you blew
in pigment that outlines your hand.
Centuries waved by, gesture sealed
with the lasting bond the sturgeon
taught us—her leaping look,
the bend of her linked spine,
saurian, ancient, enduring.

Teach me back into time
Until I know there is no time.
My hand in yours for years and years.

Our Words Are Not Our Own

We never write alone, but by a grace,
a blue silk threads our words,
makes our work both ancestor and elder,
descended of one through the other,
bound by ties that tug through time.

My words are not my own.
My words are never mine alone.
I never write, but writing comes
ink blue or pale as the spirit of the stories
who spins out a voice, a call I answer.

Place tangles with their words,
repeats them in rock's colors.
The shapes of rivers print
what we find we tell in turn,
and all unknowing, call it our own.

We never write alone, but by a ghost:
a blue spirit tangles our words
makes our work sister and brother,
related through strings we tie and tug
to pull us through the years.

Language breathes like breeze, blows words
we hear or ignore or wish we could.
We are nets and words our catch.
Or are we caught in word-woven webs,
where we tremble strings to the unknown?

Our words are not our own.
We never write alone.

Poem for Our Ojibwe Names

Those stars shine words right
into the center of the dream.

Gego zegizi kane.
Gego zegizi kane.
Maajii'am
Maajii nii'm
Majii gigidoon.

So it is when we have our names.

We will not fear.
We start to sing,
to dance, to speak.

When we did not know him
the stick man, the running man,
came jigging in our dreams.
Always in motion like a wooden toy,
he sang *"Bakenatay, Bakenatay"*
so deeply his voice was a root.

So too the woman wrapped in red wool,
whose laughter woke us, *"Chi Wabeno."*
She spoke the word for dreamers—
then teased in diminishment, *"Waban-ish."*
Still her meaning took us years to learn.

Gego zegizi kane.
Gego zegizi kane.
Maajii'am
Maajii nii'm
Majii gigidoon.

So it is when we have our names:
We will not fear.
We start to sing,
to dance, to speak.

It is not what you imagine,
no matter what you imagine.
Stars shine stories.
Words come speaking into our dreams.

In the Belly

Of my baby
I breathe rushing waters,
his element,

his blue air.
And I do not even miss the land
though sometimes we swim close enough
to see creatures very like me.
They sin and love it,
sin and forgive and go on.

In the belly of my baby
I am born and born and born
into the world a convert
whose old ways had a tang,
who wanted to walk in the dust,
tagging the powder-heeled mind.

In the belly of my baby
I have escaped the old suffering,
the self no longer dogs me, her teeth
dull as knitting needles against a silver blade
even now swinging to infant need.

In the belly of my baby
I grow another stroke, a hand
as clumsy as another set of toes.
My mouth learns to paint,
and pigment tastes the same
as ink—a bit more rich and rank.

In the belly of my baby
I am home not alone.
In the belly of my baby
I have not forgotten sin and the city,
the mission I fled, and the purge
still to come one day and spit me out.

Changeling

You grow to gold, your glow
too much honey. I look away or,
rarely, allow my eye to rest
a moment on your shining, sweet form.
Next to you, I am
so humble, such a bear,
all shag and fat and weariness.
Your mother is a bear who grew
to believe your loveliness must be
the work of tricky spirits.
Nothing else can explain the way
you hold her in your power.
Little son,
I will ask you now
because you are so easy in giving:
Forgive your mother. All her life
she has batted down the tree of bees
and barely felt the stings. Forgive her now.
What mistakes she will,
she will.

Remedy

Along the sloughs, the muskeg—
the pharmacy to the Ojibwe,
she gathered highbush fruit, pembina
for Lydia Pinkham's elixir.

They say Kookum could cure cancer,
but her remedy no one remembers.
My grandfather helped pick the cranberries,
toted sacks to the train to weigh and trade.
He learned the herbs, now disappeared
as farms plowed the wetlands down.

Do you recall this grandmother?
Powdery sweet berries in snow—
She dug wild roots, took leaves.

Did she leave asema, the snuff she carried?
Or Aunt Shyoosh's kinnikinnick?
Stripped from red willow twigs.

Her cabin swung with bundled babes,
suspended in blanket cradles from the beams
where she dried her medicines:

Prairie Sage for hemorrhage,
taproots shaped like a man's legs,
swamp tea and slippery elm,
recipes knotted into the strings
that held the stems and the twigs.

They say she could cure cancer,
that her remedy died with her.
But plants tell their own power.
She could listen. Who hears now?

Wiisah kote: The Burnt Wood People

They roll from the flames shedding,
emerge clean as wood leapt from its bark
and handsomely smooth as carvings.

This explains their knobby knees,
their knotty eyes and long-limbed ladies.
This explains their buried hearts,
their whispers in winter, their warmth.

We oaks, we old *mitigozhiig,*
rattle another season's last leaves,
hang them red against the north wind,
hold them as long as we can—
the last-leaved shelter on this savannah.

One hundred years ago, one hundred years from now,
we would stand over them, stand hard.
Let them remember their need for fire.
Fire that breaks the shell, that engenders the seed.
Fire that makes them, makes them over.

Wiisah kote or Burnt Wood is the Ojibwe name for Metis.

Basswood

Green and more green each night,
unfolding leaves, hand-sized hearts
that cleave to bright sprays.
Their scent hums across the darkness.
Honey drift brushes against us,
wets our mouths.
We speak like bees,
throats full of silky sweet:
Ozhaawashkwaabiigizi,
nininj, inde'.

Green and more green,
the Basswood groans
arms grown full with hand-waving hearts.

Ojibwe phrases: leaf-green, my hand, my heart.

The Good Woman
For Allison and Lise

The Good Woman's home makes up into beds:
pullouts that creak and plaid sofa-sleepers.
Piles of mongrel boys toss in every room,
strays with nowhere else to rest. She takes
them in, gives them each other, makes enough.

The Good Woman's screens all hang open,
or stand propped to beckon like a waved hand.
Her doors all stay unlatched, except one: behind it,
a high floral bed, or one plumped with geometrics,
and a broad or flat back she can curl her hips to,
or lock out, or leave alone.

The Good Woman's house or trailer or apartment
smells of the crockpot simmering bone and broth
and beans. It smells of foods that stretch to mouths
opening wider and wider each year.

The Good Woman wraps in wool and sits up before sun
on her porch or stoop or fire escape.
She smokes or takes tea hot or with a shot.
Across her lawn, across the street, down the sidewalk,
a path runs toward rail yard, bus station, truck stop:
all ways the boys leave, or find their way to her home.

The Good Woman holds out her hands to the blue dawn.
Beasts with heavy heads and twisting horns
bow down, breathe her in and sigh.
She has never known if this is a dream,
so she goes on waiting in the cold
for visitation, vision, benediction.

The Good Woman falls from another world, clutches
at roots and rocks and creatures as she tumbles.
Her hair rains over her face. She does not know time.
When she lands, in her pockets, in her hands,
all medicines, minerals, meat we will need,
all that the people must know to survive.

from *Fishing for Myth* (1997)

True Myth

Tell a child she is composed of parts
(her Ojibway quarters, her German half-heart)
she'll find the existence of harpies easy
to swallow. Storybook children never come close
to her mix, but manticores make great uncles,
Sphinx a cousin she'll allow, centaurs better to love
than boys—the horse part, at least, she can ride.
With a bestiary for a family album she's proud.
Her heap of blankets, her garbage grin, prove
she's descended of bears, her totem, it's true.
And that German witch with the candy roof,
that was her ancestor too. If swans can rain
white rape from heaven, then what is a girl to do?
Believe her Indian eyes, her sly French smile,
her breast with its veins skim milk blue—
She is the myth that is true.

Breaking and Entering

She kept a stash of forbidden matches,
got caught dropping splashes of wax on her bed.
Iced-over sidewalks, the ones I loved to skim,
she cracked with her hard heel. All I got was
water welling up where she walked. Still, I followed
through the shards, saw her jump in some boy's car.
She started the dream—a storm with flat hands
bangs on all the windows, a storm in a green gown
with rain-dark hair. This girl, who wouldn't lift
her gray eyes to her mother's gaze, would make love
in old farmhouses, on abandoned boxsprings,
on scoured linoleum, in rusted bathtubs,
junked trucks along windbreaks.
She broke in, she told me, not to love
those boys, but to melt them down,
look them in the eye and crack their glaze.
She started the dream—a storm pries the edge
off the roof, lifts my lids, glares at me with a gray eye
that strikes on love, that can get past all human walls.

The Red River of the North

Like all water it cares for its creatures.
They draw each drop they drink from it,
and when they paw the ground or cut
a furrow in a field, river scent comes up.
They trust its unusual course, the path
lapping flat as a tongue to Canada.
In their veins there's a pull
direct as that flow: North,
forever, even through winter
frozen four-feet thick or breaking
in spring, surging ice chunks big as cars—
it brims in ditches, on roads, when it seeps
into fields, leaves June sloughs thick with cattails
that brown and explode as the dry July wind
whips fields into thirty-foot spires of dust.
Drought drives the river underground,
exposes its bed: bottles and jars,
stranded fish sloughing their flesh,
washboards and tires,
the river's bone and core.
People pick about for souvenirs.
Though the bullhead's flesh tastes muddy,
boys pull squirming netfuls from puddles.
And the snapping turtles, all plates and claws,
some big enough for a child to stand on,
their hundred-year-old faces
sunk in rings of wrinkles,
bask peacefully on strands between ponds,
while beside the bridge abutment
young drunks park in their pickups.
They have come for the snappers,
easy catches in a river so low.
They break branches, lurch toward
the turtles whose jaws lock,

clench the sticks, hold
and hold even as they are lifted,
even at the shock of the hatchet.
Shell trunks trudge headless,
straight toward the water.
The young men laugh long laughs
throwing their own heads back.
They do not notice the sky go green,
hung with hail teats to the west.
Herons, blue as smoke, rise,
seek higher ground. In the muck,
the men gather turtles, toss the bodies
in the truckbed where reflex
makes the reptiles' nails kick
a scratching call the river answers
in a flash of rain. The trickle swells,
sucks ankle deep, whorls to the men's lips,
pours and rushes into them, washes them
until they drink a first watery breath
in a world of heron and catfish—
This is the river ignorant of banks
and dikes and bridges, swimming back,
wanting only to rise and rise beyond
what binding or straightening inflicts,
wanting to fill its creatures
with insistent murkiness, the cold urge
that pumps in every pulse: North
the way our blood goes in its sleep,
the way all things must go
in shells or scales or feathers.

Oxbow

To Asiganak

Go to one of those little islands on the prairie
that haven't been broken and stitched with wheat—
Where the river has swung a loop
out of its ancient path—
Where mounds of earth along the slough
form sculptures only the sky can see—
Watch meadowlarks thrust
their banded throats up and warble
their yellow heads off—
Listen as yellow-headed blackbirds,
bobbing on reeds, ricochet their untuned calls—
Taste juneberry, chokecherry, wild plum—
See how the redwing blackbirds took
their showy epaulettes
from the high-bush cranberries—
Hear how that tart fruit
cracked their voices for good.

Rich Hour
Gulf War, 1991

Starlings, those blue-black and shaggy birds whose feathers seem secondhand, starlings I've never liked. But for now, because the warring world beyond this courtyard has gone grey, lit with silent twisting flashes, for now I am happy they stay.

True, starlings kill treetops, drop their messes lavishly, even where they eat. Still, they're social birds, seldom alone, always regarding one another with quick birdy glances, always whistling "whew" as in "that was a close one"—to which I always whisper, "yes, it was."

Perhaps I'm deluded, only imagining this blue rectangle of sky is the last door anywhere left open to the sun. Why else would the birds flock here?

A mockingbird rushes the starlings. To spite them she opens the fountain of her throat and the sweetest sounds known to birds come out: the all-clear signal, the *love here* signal, the universal call to drink the dew before the day does.

I am not distracted. I've only grown full with war and these milling starlings, these indifferent street folk bored by the mockingbird's lulling, evening voice.

Now I see, war works like grief—makes vision sharp, more rare, so it is clear I have always been here, in this courtyard, with these starlings scrabbling at my feet, with the mockingbird's words printed on air, the blue door closing above me.

One Girl

These were decent people,
publishing the salaries of public employees,
their indiscretions and local tragedies.
They came from a land of hunger
to this place protected from storms
according to an old Indian blessing.
It seemed everyone made way:
the old ones who called the land holy;
even the ancient lake drew back her flat
skirt of waters leaving good black earth.
They built up the lowlands, drained ponds,
pushed back the river banks to plant grain.
They made this place rise like bread.

One Girl walked right out of the earth.
She stood on their bridge telling their sons
the story of the river in its own language.
Those boys returned home silent or,
against their mother's glances, tried words
that broke and stumbled like water over rocks.
One Girl stood during storms on their bridge,
watching funnels draw up into clouds passing close,
as though she had come to take that leftover blessing,
let the tornado slam like a freight train down main street.

They drove her out of town through their graveyard,
through stubbled wheat by the water tower.
And then did they see? Her heart cracked open,
a sack of hard yellow feed, spilled for crows to pick.
The black wind wrapped her body.
Her tattered cries flapped away like birds.
Now, to boys who would speak it,
even her name sounds far away.

Human Map

You will be happy to know someone has asked our cells to tell,
in their own bloody language, whether or not all Indian tribes
descend from a single group migrated from Asia.

Your own body contains the answers and the map: "Hidden within
the DNA of each human being is a record of that person's ethnic history."
Just one drop can read like a mystery.

All the way back to "humanity's dim evolutionary past,"
without a flashlight, scientists can trace
"the ancient migrations and ancestral intermixings
that have shaped every tribe and culture on Earth."

Still, it's too late to test Sky Woman, whose breath of life exists
in all creatures, or Thought Woman, who imagines us even now,
or any of the First Beings who survived by tricks.

Too late, so they will have to settle for *your* blood.

Some tribal jokesters call this *The Vampire Project*. Rumor has it
donations need no consent and any clinic might be in on it—so
go ahead—Give Blood! It's your civic duty.

Anthropologists, our old friends, support this "needy and urgent
cause." And who knows? You may be one of the "HIP people"
(Historically Interesting Population)
who, they note, are vanishing at an alarming rate.

Vanishing? They make it sound so passive, as if whole peoples
simply fade away.

You say you won't go to the blood drive? But the needle's nothing
new. Bloodshed always determines who inherits a patch of earth.

Even they admit their findings might be used to support
"increasingly incendiary claims of land tenure in ethnic disputes."

Do not fear this genetic tattooing—if they keep it up long enough,
they will discover we all belong to one mother.

Scholars insist "the concept of race long ago lost its scientific
validity." And you know how well the general public embraces
these subtle distinctions and complex genetic notions.
Soon racism *as we know it* will end.

Whether we help them or not is no matter. Our blood will out.
Our bodies' code will crack. They will have their map.

All quotes from "By Analyzing DNA Samples from 400 Ethnic Groups, Scientists
Could Reconstruct Human History," Boyce Rensberger, Washington Post, March
15–21, 1993.

The Pond

Baltimore's flowers go off like fireworks.
Azaleas buzz in colors too hot for our eyes.
You take me to a pond with a cooling fountain,
a bronze child leaping across lilypads. I'm amazed
when you stamp your feet and the koi rise to be fed.
We have come to release an overgrown fantail goldfish.
She slips from the plastic bag, and glimmers above dull coins,
disappears into waters as filled with wishes as marriage.
I press a penny to my lips, toss it in the depths.

Catch and release, catch and release—we have loved
this way for years. That day at the pond repeats,
it seems. The splashing child never
ages, our reflections always waver and you
keep stamping at the edge of that pond until
hundreds of fish churn at its surface,
bubbling up with wishes at their lips,
all the best, all for you.

Fat in America

This is no joke. She is fat and happy in the U.S.A. The kind of woman who always has plenty of loving men—not just perverts either. You are thinking that she can't be all that fat. Well, she is. There are folds of flesh at the back of her neck—her half-moon cheeks swallow her eyes—her eyes are olives sunk in the whole wheat dough—her chin doubles when she laughs, and wobbles when she talks—her shoulders are broad and sold as XXL men's. Her breasts are vast. There is no other way to say it. Unless we say they are globes of warmth or that she would nurse nations. Oh, she has held a lover's head between them and covered all but his bald spot. And yet she has a waist, still obviously indented beneath a rich ring of belly—her hips rise biblically (mounds, doves, wheat, hills) nothing is fertile enough to describe them, except the Great Plains where she was born. Yes, her hips are like cropland. And the valley between? A gorgeous secret place, a gorge of ferns and falls—her thighs are sacks of grain, a harvest—her calves carved timbers, marble sculpture. And her feet? Ah! These are the platforms of faith—holy and round and strong.

That Green Night

"The next evening they slept under the stars again.
This time those two fellows came and took them up to
their hut above the clouds."

—STAR HUSBAND STORY, TOLD BY JULIA BADGER IN 1944

Even now, she could give him
a look that would shake him
make him roll rrrs through his teeth
like her wolf-mate, sitting there
in his leather office chair,
his awards breathless under glass,
his desk pressed to the wall.

When she thinks of how she loved him—
foolish, she knows, to thank him,
years after all the sparky hot stuff
that drove them down a river road hung
with a long-limbed painter's trees.

Did he know how, around that fire,
singing Indian songs, her cheek pressed
to the words humming in his throat,
his arm low on her back—Did he know
how she gave up faith in everything
but the green night around them—
floating against him, his blanket edge
tight around them both, her feet barely
skimming the grass, swaying for hours
until the sky stepped down, opened his bright arms—
Did he know how many years that one night held her?
If he had let go any sooner she would have flown

                        beyond earth with those stars.

Flickers

Abandoned town on the border, I wait
in tedious drilling noise. Flickers,
my sister birds, try a hole. Grub-full
and greedy, they ignore me. Fine, I say,
just fine. When have those birds ever

waited for me? What's in that hole for me?
It is hot while I stalk Flickers for feathers—
red and yellow shafts I mean to collect
for prayer fans. Hen-bodied, they would plummet

so easily. It's a pity they act so disappointed in love.
They make their mates sob sad wet notes that move
them to nest in dead wood. I watch, my gaze still, hot.

Ah! Their wings burn right past me.
One eyes me: the sun in a crushing black rock.
She blots me bone dry, sends me dreaming
through a red and yellow thirst—
this prayer they will teach me.

Sex in the Desert

My brain won't admit the desert at first—won't comprehend
heat like a seizure. *Empty* seems too potent a word

for weeks of cloudless unmerciful sky—
Finally, a storm strides toward the Pipe Organ Mountains;

its first drops, big as quarters, sting my skin,
then comes a scent; burned sugar, burning spice—

My blood goes crazy for the sound of wet on dry.
I huff, I snort, I run around the courtyard yelling,

hey, hey, it's raining! My breath comes in deep and high.
Little bugs crawl from every crack in the earth—

The desert is creaking open, spreading herself for love.
Her richness rises in clouds of dust kicked up by rain,

her smell is burned sugar, butterscotch, cinnamon on fire.
The scene's embarrassing, primal: Earth ravaged by Father Sky.

Leaves beat back the rain with a noise like frantic birds;
violent showers send me under a tree bent by water.

The cuckoos and grackles in the branches hoot in a frenzy,
groaning and chortling, letting out manic sexual cries—

Then it is over. The desert has had enough already.
She just reclines, all wet, delicately steaming as she dries.

Father Sky shags off, withdraws over the desolate mountains.
The cuckoos rise to the bush tops, let out a collective sigh.

Hopi Prophet Chooses a Pop

The light and air? They are mountain-perfect, in Taos, near some tennis courts, our conference room door open, all that clear sun whisking in while we carry on our hot debate in a think-tank of artists and healers.

We are out to save the world.

My own insomniac clarity lets me see how powerfully ordinary he is, that Hopi elder, who says humbly, simply, what we somehow knew was true all along. How sweet his words, clear water rushing cold to our lips, all the drink we'd ever need—

Until coffee break.

The foam cups lined up, the donuts piled up like a stack of spare tires—I go outside and find him there, nothing between us but bright air and a tonal vending machine.

That junk's not for me, he says, glancing back to the foyer door, now blocked by three stainless coffee urns.

No, I reply.

He pats his pockets for glasses. The vending machine sighs. We approach it respectfully, as teens do jukeboxes, as gamblers do slots. *Read me what she's got,* he squints through yellowed lenses. I will admit it: I hope to divine what he'd like, that my right choice will somehow reflect how much of his teaching I get—*There's the sparkling water,* I try, jingling my change.

No response but the slight expectant shift.

There's apple juice, veggie cocktail? I ask, thinking he'd like something natural. *Or Bubble Up, ginger ale, cream soda?* I am on a roll call of beverages: *Root beer, Crush, Nehi?* As if that machine contains all the liquids ever canned by human hands, I list: *Tonic, sarsaparilla, lemon-lime, Coco-yahoo soda, diet this, caffeine-free that, and all your regular colas.*

I appeal to the horizon, source inspiration, and make one last certain offer: *Mountain Dew.*

A pause, but no, no response.

Finally I feed in dimes. The coin slot gulps, my own favorite choice rolls down. Just then the button flashes—machine's all out—And then, of course, he cries: *That's right! That's right! That one I like. I'll take that Doctor Pop.*

Wearing Indian Jewelry

I was wondering why that guy
wore the blanket coat, bone choker, rock
watch, woven buckle, quilled Stetson—
I was wondering why he wore
that beaded vest, like a ledger drawing
or a Winter Count, its skinny figure
forever sneaking after two bison
around belly to back,
around back to belly—
I was wondering why, when he said,
I wear these getups every day—
Every day, because these things
are sacred, these things are prayer.

Then I knew I could live this life
if I had blue horses
painted around and around me,
shells and beads like rain in my ear
praying *Prairie open in me*
at stoplight, hard city, last call, bank line,
coffee break, shopping cart, keycode,
Prairie open in me
Prairie open in me
every day every day every day.

Turtle Rattle
For Val

That prayer shaker hanging there, I've never rattled.
A gift from Billy, up in Oklahoma, I was flattered.
But to shake it, I should make a song I can't yet grasp
about its plates, like moons, a calendar of the past,
a year we would erase, since our friend lost her battle,
sunk dark in Alaska, where she drank a death so hard—
hard to stop the picture, yet we will not say the word,
at least not until our songs can make it matter.
Then we will chant, count years, and raise the rattle.

Ants died working hard to clean flesh from inside
this turtle. Those little sisters now a part
of the noise—dried ants and small stones scatter
when I shift the shell. I would shake it so hard,
hard for me to pick it up though, to shake, shake.
Stones fall through me, break into ants, shatter.
Rhythm hits us hardest, makes us sadder.
Easier to shy away in rhyme and prattle, prattle.

Sing the truth. Shake a prayer with turtle, turtle
whose endurance at its root means hard, hard.
We are stone, we go on, our two hands lift the rattle.

Translation

Enter the simple landscape
of snow on broken fields,
trust those lines it gives up:
two narrow trees, a dip in the land,
a farmhouse heaved into itself, abandoned.
We go to the doorway, no further—
beyond the threshold we would step into air.
The floor, collapsed as if a bomb dropped,
framed by walls hung with ghostly
impressions of pictures long gone,
tells of a great force. We imagine
that a tornado, noisy as a pressure cooker
caught in the chimney, brought the floor down.
No one home to open east windows,
front door, storm doors to the cellar.
This is a place forever falling on itself,
a story we should recognize.
But we turn in that doorway, face
the blue glare, the horizon flat out like a lover
pressing close to fields, rails, road.
We stare until the train tracks
trick our eyes, collide at the edge of sight.
We should go to them, lie side to side,
our ears to the rails, hear the low singing,
smell iron become a flat yet bitter taste.
And if we lie there until the train
makes an eye of light in the sky,
and if we stand or stumble
while the train spins the ground away,
if we watch until we are certain
there is no meeting of those tracks,
would we still think we could break
the law of a land with parallels so vast?
As if we are stories mere touch can translate.

Animoosh

A girl surrounded by brothers
has to have a dream. Mine
was to live deep in green woods
near a stream with a dog to protect me.
Not the family dog, that pile of lint
who licked and begged, but some dream
dog who would mysteriously appear.
Heroic canine—swift as a Greyhound,
she'd share her kill. Her markings
would be expressive as a Shepherd's
mobile brows and a smiling muzzle.
She'd be velvet-pelted as a Bulldog
and as big-jawed to pull me from sink holes,
mud slides. I'd call the mutt Annie,
and when we rested on the cold earth,
breathing the same raw-rabbit breath,
far from home, darkness creaking about us,
Annie's ears twitching, tail swishing—
we could howl all our loneliness into the world.

I was sure the dog would come from my dream.
With my back to the shadow edge of the shelter belt,
I would stare until I saw her—always just beyond me,
bounding through the long field of goldenrod and sun.

Animoosh is Ojibwe for dog.

TV News: Detox Closed

No comment, just image after image
of the frontline troops
in the Alcohol and Indian War—
The camera gives us back a day
with a band of merry tribal drunks
who, by midnight, will wind up
in the ER, getting tested and typed,
paying in blood for a night's stay.

On a red carpeted stairway,
a TV newsman stands,
a polished bastard of a banister
glides thirty feet of wood
under his hand. He gazes
from the tube, ironic, amused,
saying since Detox closed
taxpayers spent $300 per inebriate
on nightly emergency treatment.

He gestures meaningfully
at the parquet floor;
the chandelier winks
at his sick little joke
about the nightly rate
of a honeymoon suite,
which somehow explains
why he's reporting on Detox
from the foyer of a luxury hotel.

Yeah, I'd like to see those guys
put up for a night in the Ritz.
What a party! Sneak in some old friends,
by the end of the night we'd drop
the taxpayer's cost to, say,
thirty dollars a head.

More video images, more faces.
I peer at them as through water,
wondering who were on the land.
Street Chiefs, I've heard them called,
a name whose honor is earned backward,
unspoken by the time it's deserved.
Heroes do return, yes, healed like warriors,
but these on TV are still so far away.

There is a battle in a distant country
where breath and drink are twins.
Each swallow, you pull toward that world
whose element is alcohol, not air.
Tilt the bottle to see the entrance,
a hole at the top of the sky, bright as sun,
the glass lip a tunnel toward that land
whose voice always provokes you
come on, come on
where you belong—
Now tell me you wouldn't go.

The Visible Woman

was her name—
the plastic model of anatomy,
who wanted to be cousin to dolls.
Her larger size, and lashless eyeballs
washed over by a face sheer as a wave,
her viewable puzzles of lifelike entrails
encased in a skin clear of texture and detail,
terrorized Barbie, even Ken.
Alien, indiscreet, her vitals all too obvious,
she was unwelcome, fled from when she called.
Building block doorways fell as she entered.
Mute, stiff, indelicate, she lacked Barbie's
parting lips, swivel hips, and discreet, polished nails.
Her hands, fused into fingerless, scallop-edged cups
on stiff arms held waist-high, palms up,
offered an awful embrace of kinship.

Do you see how any day your inside might out?
You expect to ripen to that blonde plastic body,
while already your skin pures, lifting like a mist,
rinsing free to your most visible core
where blue and red branches, artery and vein,
etch surely to your heart, from your heart, and open-armed,
thumb-pinkie-index-fore meld to raise you like wings.

Future Debris

The typical object up there is about the size of a filing cabinet.
—From "Space Junk a Danger to Launches,"
Johns Hopkins Gazette, August 23, 1988

Until he died we thought our neighbor dull.
Now he's a distant point of light.
His cremated body orbits low
in its reflectorized canister creating
what the space burial firm called
"a twinkling reminder of the loved one."
There's a wheel chart to map his course.
Nights we go around back of the house,
gaze at what little true sky winks
through the haze of debris.
It amazes me and is a relief, really,
not to have the whole universe
smack up against me like a wall.
All my life I've strained to comprehend
planets and motion, all the unending
that's been clouded, obscured
by the detritus humans seem to produce
naturally, ink to the squid, protective
cloak through which we cannot see
and therefore feel we are not seen.
Some night, a little girl, who will know
only tame animals, city trees, will listen
to my tales of wilderness and game.
I'll hold her up so she basks in the glint
of celestial jetsam. She will spread her hands,
reach for the bright flecks, ask if they are wild.
Lying to the child, I'll say they are. Then the filing
cabinets, ah, they'll glimmer like stars!

Sense

Streetlights blur, elongated
on the wet reflective pavement.
Under one umbrella, two people
guided by white canes, catch
the rush of a traffic wave, splash
across to the gutter, and are safe.

At the market a deaf couple
sign as they shop the aisles.
They turn from each other, unaware,
and in a moment find their fingers
telling words to air. The man laughs,
thrusts his still-speaking hands into her hair.

Here, now, darkness wraps our bodies.
We float silent, lightless, except where
a slat broken in the blind plays
light across your chest, my neck.
The heat that rises from our skin
gives us voice and vision. You trace
a curve and dot along the plane of my cheek.
My mouth against your collarbone moves
an answer to your question mark: yes, yes.

Notes

I provided author's notes for my second and third books. They were created with the primary intention of encouraging students (and those whose curiosity is piqued by my subject matter) to investigate my references further. I've provided notes here for the new work in *Cell Traffic* as well as original (and updated) notes from the works published earlier. Further comment, links to articles, and information that inspires my writing can be found at HeidErdrich.com.

Notes to *Cell Traffic*

The title of this collection, *Cell Traffic*, suggests movement, small units passing back and forth, busy telecommunications, internet chatter and terrorist groups, the sale or traffic in DNA or body parts or bones, indigenousness and ancestral inheritance, migration through procreation, and other biological processes. I mean for all of these notions and more to come into play for readers, not just with the new poems collected here but as a through-line carried, to some extent, throughout all of my books.

That said, *Cell Traffic* takes its title from the term based on the scientific fact that cells have been found to move from the fetal body to the maternal body and vice versa. The result of cell traffic is called microchimerism, the existence of cells within us that are not genetically our own. The poems "Microchimerism" and "Little Souvenirs from the DNA Trading Post," as well as others in this collection, include quotes from and make reference to a 2002 paper by Dr. Judith G. Hall and from a profile of Dr. Diana Bianchi in *Tufts Medicine*, 2005, written by Bruce Morgan (editor). You can see the profile of Dr. Bianchi based on Morgan's article at: http://www.tufts.edu/home/feature/?p=bianchi and, if you first sign in, you can read the 2002 presentation titled "Fetal Determinants of Adult Health" by Dr. Judith G. Hall, at http://www.medscape.org/viewarticle/432305.

My younger sister Angie Erdrich is a human being of great integrity, a gifted visual artist, and a mother of four. She is a pediatrician who has worked with American Indian populations her entire career. We have Angie to thank (or blame) for turning me on to the fascinating world of cell traffic. She sent me an article about maternal-fetal cell traffic research, and the more I learned, the more I felt that knowledge of how our cells act answered basic spiritual questions and upheld my own intuitions about my connections to my children. It seems a hopeful field of study, too, as the role of fetal cells in protecting the mother is becoming understood, or at least written about, in ways that strike me as feminist and positive. More is known about other kinds of microchimerism all the time—all of it just too darn interesting. Sometimes a person, born singularly, can be a blood chimera (hence the title "Blood Chimera")—meaning the person's blood type is not straightforwardly his or hers but may be the result of having once been, at a very early stage of fetal development, a twin—to put a complex thing very simply. I read about such things in, among other sources, an article written by Claire Ainsworth titled "The Stranger Within" (*New Scientist*, November 2003)—the article quoted on the epigraph page opening this book.

As in my earlier work, popular notions of science often trigger my poetry in *Cell Traffic*. The poem "Thrifty Gene, Lucky Gene" responds to the idea of the "thrifty gene," described as the gene that allows some people to gain weight easily. "Brain Scan" was written after I heard Dr. Amen (author of *Change Your Brain, Change Your Life*) on public television describing how brain imaging could be used to help relationships. "Mitochondrial Eve" was written some time between 2007 and 2010. The talented Gwen Westerman wrote a poem of the same title and I hope I did not steal it from her. Perhaps we share a mitochondrial mother and the idea was within us both? In any case, "mitochondrial Eve" is a phrase I've heard used to describe the original genetic ancestor from whom all humanity is said to descend. Such science is constantly debunked and debated and, at one point, reports that there were actually seven mitochondrial Eves made the news. My poem "Seven Mothers" also makes reference to the idea of the original seven genetic mothers. The subject is worth an internet search. There are a few curious articles speculating on how mitochondrial research influenced the television remake of *Battlestar Galactica*, a series I respond to tangentially in several poems. The poem "DNA Tribes" remarks on pop-up ads that appear uncannily when I am trying to do serious research on Native American subjects or if I exchange gmails with anyone who works for a Native American organization. Yes, I have changed my settings to avoid such intrusions, but not before they gave me a poem.

My obsessions are not, however, limited to the quirky beauty of science. For several years I have been working with American Indian visual artists, a fact reflected in a few poems here. Jim Denomie paints rabbits and I thought of his paintings and his ideas about rabbits (he calls them "evening eagles") while I wrote several poems with rabbits in them, one of which begins this collection. Norval Morrisseau was one of the original painters of the Woodland school of indigenous artists. His style is vivid and spiritual and contains references to the Ojibwe symbol system. Frank Big Bear, to whom "Paint These Streets" is dedicated, is also an Ojibwe artist whose brilliant pencil drawings and paintings I have had the privilege to present during my time as curator at All My Relations Arts in Minneapolis.

Although I generally do not provide ethnographic notes, it might help to know a wiindigo (commonly spelled windigo) is a cannibal spirit much storied by Ojibwe people; a chimera, another monster, is not of Ojibwe origin. The names for both monsters, however, appeared in the top 30 percent of searches in a popular online dictionary one week in 2011.

Often my poems are conflations of the actual with the imagined. This bothers a few people (some people I dearly love and respect as thinkers and poets) who have encouraged me to frame my intellectual imaginings with personal perspective. The poems that consciously place a self (and even now I won't quite say it is myself) within *Cell Traffic* carry titles that begin with "Now," and "Own Your Own" and have something to do with my life. That said, the initials in "Own Your Own: Cellular Changes" do not reflect actual surgeons' names. Also, although I recently found out my blood is a tad unusual, I am not a Blood Chimera, as far as I know.

Several of the prose poems included here were created in collaborative circumstances. "Dancer Origin Story" and "Twin Dancers" were created as I acted as creative consultant to dancer and choreographer Sally Rousse, a lifelong friend, during the creation of her ballet *Paramount to My Footage*. The prose poems featuring Star Hawk were created as part of Talking Images, a reading series at Soap Factory gallery in Minneapolis that asks writers to respond to exhibits. The installation that inspired my work, *New Land of Milk and Honey*, created images of a utopian society focused on knitting.

Notes to *National Monuments*

"Guidelines for the Treatment of Sacred Objects" slightly spoofs NAGPRA, the Native American Graves Protection and Repatriation Act.

Grand Portage is one of two national monuments in my home state of Minnesota.

"Some Elsie": All the Elsie poems refer to William Carlos Williams's poem "To Elsie."

"The Lone Reader and Tonchee Fistfight in Pages" borrows on a title by Sherman Alexie.

"Body Works" does not refer to the show of this title, but another much like it.

"Kennewick Man Tells All," and all three poems in the Kennewick Man series were influenced by an essay by Susan J. Crawford in Repatriation Reader.

"Prisoner No. 280" refers to the French queen, Marie Antoinette.

"Girl of Lightning" contains a complex set of responses to readings about the display of child mummies in South America. A discussion board on the subject posted by "American Renaissance," prompted outrageously racist responses. The discussion posts have since been taken down.

Notes to The Mother's Tongue

The Mother's Tongue was published with two contextual pieces: a long prose poem/essay not included here and brief author's notes. Those notes, in an abbreviated form, appear below along with an additional new note on Anishaabemowin (Ojibwe language) use.

"This Body, The River" is inspired by a Jim Denomie painting.

"Kookum" is a Mechif/Metis word from the Ojibwe, Nokomis, meaning grandmother. This is what my mother called her grandmother and how she referred to her when telling stories.

"Remedy" mentions Lydia Pinkham's elixir, a patent medicine for "female problems" that was composed of cranberry and other plants, often gathered by American Indian women including my great-grandmother Eliza Gourneau.

The dictionary I used for Anishinaabe language spelling was *A Concise Dictionary of Minnesota Ojibwe,* edited by John Nichols and Earl Nyholm, University of Minnesota Press,1995. My use of Anishinaabe language was proofed by several people adept in the language. However, oddities and mistakes are not to be blamed on my teachers. In some instances, and purposely, I used a slight variant on a word that drew it closer to the dialect of my ancestors. In other instances words came to me in dreams and I tried to spell them as correctly as possible. I prefaced *The Mother's Tongue* with a note that I am a rude beginner in studying the Anishinaabe language. Also, I thanked my teachers and language table leaders, and I thanked the spirit of the language in Anishinaabemowin (the Ojibwe language) as I do now. Miigwech. My poetry collection *The Mother's Tongue* was meant to draw a connection between motherhood as the teaching of language and the recovery and revitalization of indigenous languages, particularly Anishinaabemowin.

Notes to *Fishing for Myth*

Fishing for Myth was published without author's notes. One item I would like to clarify at this point is that most of the myths I tell in this work are personal and arrived at by creative means. These are not traditional Ojibwe stories in any way—although a few poems do reference sacred stories from a number of cultures. Some of these references are clear from the epigraph to the poem, as when I incorporate the Julia Badger quote in "That Green Night." Also of note, some of the poems in this first book began my practice of reading science-writing as inspiration. Finally, two poems from *Fishing for Myth* included here were drafted in my college days at Dartmouth and revised ten years later for the book's publication in 1997. Those poems are "Red River of the North" and "Translation." So keep revising, poetry students!

About the Author

Winner of the 2009 Minnesota Book Award for *National Monuments* (Michigan State University Press), Heid E. Erdrich has authored four books of poetry and co-edited *Sister Nations: Native American Women on Community,* an anthology. Heid grew up in Wahpeton, North Dakota, and is Ojibwe, enrolled at Turtle Mountain. She graduated from Dartmouth College and The Johns Hopkins University. Heid taught college writing for two decades, including many years as a tenured professor. Since 2007, Heid has worked with American Indian visual artists as an arts advocate and a curator. In 2010 she founded Wiigwaas Press to publish Ojibwe language books. She travels often to colleges, universities, and libraries as a visiting author, and she offers writing workshops regularly. Heid's current project is a cookbook from the indigenous food movement in Minnesota.